Thomas Russell Hillier McClatchie

Japanese Plays

versified

Thomas Russell Hillier McClatchie

Japanese Plays
versified

ISBN/EAN: 9783337164379

Printed in Europe, USA, Canada, Australia, Japan

Cover: Foto ©ninafisch / pixelio.de

More available books at **www.hansebooks.com**

Japanese Plays,

(Versified.)

BY

Thomas R. H. McClatchie,

Interpreter,

H. B. M.'s Consular Service, Japan.

WITH ILLUSTRATIONS,

Drawn and Engraved by Japanese Artists.

YOKOHAMA:
1879.

PREFACE.

THE following rhymes must not be taken as translations of the dramas to which they allude. They are merely efforts to sketch, in a cursory manner, the general outline of the plots of those dramas, for the especial benefit of Western readers. The great improvements that have recently been introduced on the Japanese stage have naturally given rise to a desire on the part of many foreign residents here to make some slight acquaintance with the general style and character of the plays represented. A Japanese play, as a rule, lasts for many hours, and it is questionable whether it would, if literally and fully translated, possess any interest for the foreign reader. The plan here followed has been to select one personage as the hero or heroine, and to give an outline of those scenes only in which that particular personage appears; for this reason several of these rhymes are termed 'Fragments.' A Japanese audience, though certainly sympathetic, differs considerably from a foreign one: the spectators here are by no means averse to showing their amusement when an unfortunate woman is murdered by mistake, but are easily moved to tears when the murderer finally commits suicide after a long speech garnished with grandiloquent allusions to the spirit of 'loyalty' that caused him to perpetrate the

PREFACE.

outrage in the first instance. Thus, in endeavoring to versify these plays, no style has appeared so apt as that of the "Ingoldsby Legends,"—that delightful mixture of pathos and bathos, of true poetic expression and of jingling rhyme. This idea has been kept in view throughout.

The illustrations are from the clever pencil of Mr. Tachibana Unga, an official of the Imperial Japanese Military Department, and have been cut on blocks by Hisanaga Heizô, a wood-engraver of Tôkiô.

All these rhymes have already appeared in the columns of the "Japan Daily Herald," at Yokohama, and it is to the kind courtesy of the editor of that journal that the author is indebted for permission to reprint them in separate form.

Yokohama, August, 1879.

CONTENTS.

	PAGE.
HAYANO KAMPEI	2
THE FATAL ERROR	20
LADY KOKONOYÉ	46
THE HAUNTED MANSION	67
THE ENCHANTED PALACE	93
THE FENCING MASTER	115

LIST OF ILLUSTRATIONS.

		TO FACE PAGE.
1.—A Japanese Theatre		*Frontispiece*
2.—Death of Yoichibei		8
3.—Suicide of Kampei		15
4.—The Councillor and Kwansuke		29
5.—The Attack on the Train		37
6.—The Councillor's Visit		42
7.—Lady Kokonoye		49
8.—The False Envoy		58
9.—In Ambush		63
10.—The Haunted Well		77
11.—The Conspirators		79
12.—Evil Tidings		83
13.—The Bishop and his Retainers		98
14.—The Merry-makers		106
15.—The Bishop in Danger		110
16.—Jiubei's Madness		123
17.—The Fencing Bout		128
18.—The Riddle Solved		133

HAYANO KAMPEI.

THIS is a fragment from the play of the "Chiushingura," one of the most popular, and certainly the best known of Japanese dramas. The tale of the "Forty-seven Rônin" who avenged the death of their feudal liege is, no doubt, sufficiently well known to our readers through the medium of Mr. A. B. Mitford's "Tales of Old Japan." The drama itself is exceedingly long, but amongst all its varied scenes there is scarcely one that so thoroughly engrosses the attention of a Japanese audience as that on which is founded the following rhyme. The name of Hayano Kampei is inseparably associated with the deeds of the valiant forty-seven; and tradition has it that, as a reward for his loyalty to the interests of his lord's house, the fatal purse that was the indirect cause of his death was afterwards borne by one of the Rônin in their midnight onslaught on the mansion of their foe. But we will let the tale speak for itself.

ayano ampei ;

A Fragment from the Japanese Play of the "Chiushingura," (the "Forty-seven Rônin,")—as Performed at the Shimabara Theatre, Tôkiô, 1875.

YOICHIBEI, leading a woodcutter's life,
    Is bless'd with that treasure,—a virtuous wife ;
And, as happens with most married folks who agree,
The pair are as happy as happy can be :
    Though lowly their lot,
    And humble their cot,
Though the winds may blow chill, or the sun beat
    down hot,—
Yet little they reck, in their mountain retreat,
Of the strife of the city that lies at their feet ;
Content with each other, they dwell in the hills,
Each halving the other's joys, labours, and ills ;
    Their pleasures they share,
    Their trials they bear,
And, in fact, all their neighbours are wont to declare,
That they never yet saw such a jolly old pair !

Their marriage is blessed with one child,—(who'd
    have thought her
A woodcutter's offspring ?)—a beautiful daughter ;—

So fair and so stately, for provinces round
No Japanese damsel her equal was found;
So dutiful, charming, so gay and so free,
And possessed, above all, with such happy *esprit;*
Her tasty attire might a Shôguness vex,—
"*Munditiis,*" Horace would tell us, "*simplex!*"
What wonder that envious neighbours should sneer,
When her form they espy, or her praises they hear!
What wonder the love-sick young men of the plain
Should vie with each other her favour to gain!
With suitors enough and to spare was she blessed,
But wisely she chose, and her love she confessed
To him who of all the swains loved her the best;
And she soon 'named the day,' (tho' with tremulous
    voice)
To Hayano Kampei, the youth of her choice!

  The knot is tied,
  The blushing bride
   Must quit her mountain home,
  Must leave behind
  Her parents kind,
   In other lands to roam.
But Hayano whispers soft words in her ear,—
Dispels all her fears, bids her be of good cheer,—
And so whisks her off, and they both journey down
To Akô, in Banshiu, his lord's castle-town.

Now his chief, my lord Asano,—none need be told,—
Is of lineage ancient, a *daimió*[1] bold;
But somehow or other he gets in a scrape,

---

1. *Daimió,*—a territorial noble.

In a " regular fix,"—there's no chance of escape,—
So he puts a bold face on't, displays no surprise,
But commits *hara-kiri*,² and quietly dies!
Of course his retainers all growl like the deuce
At losing their incomes,—but that's of no use;
So to North, West, and East they all scatter away,
And the Hayanos go with their parents to stay.

    What need to recall
    All the ills that befall,—
How poverty holds the poor folks in its thrall,—
How times, when once bad, still go on growing worse,
(While the victims, despondent, now pray and now
    curse)
Till at last they're as bad as they ever can be,
And the woodcutter's family's quite ' up a tree;'—
Well, to cut matters short, then, it happens one day
That our household is found in a very bad way;
    Not a cash, not a ' red
    Cent,' or morsel of bread,—
And a wicked thought enters Yoichibei's head!
He beckons his wife, and a confabulation
Ensues, in low tones, 'bout their sore tribulation.
" Our daughter," says he, " is a regular prize,—
" A damsel so charming, so lovely, so wise,
" Is a rarity,—and, wife, I'm sure you'll agree,
" As we've reared *her* since she was a child on your knee,
" That she now should help *us*, and—though you
    needn't tell her—
"'Twould be a good stroke could we manage to sell
    her!

---

2. *Hara-kiri*,—suicide by disembowelment.

"'Twould enable us now to get something to eat,
"And in time we perhaps might yet fall on our feet."
(Don't faint, gentle reader, nor call it a sin,
That a father should deal in his own kith and kin;
You've been brought up, perhaps, in a different school,
In Japan, though, I hear, it's according to rule!)
    Now, Yoichibei's wife
    Wished to save her own life,
But she stood in great dread of a family strife;
To her husband's proposal, then, all she could say
Was,—" To-morrow, when Hayano's out of the way!"

Yoichibei rises next morn with the sun,
Sees Hayano off with his dog and his gun,
    And bids him take heed
    Of himself, then with speed
Dons cloak and hat, pauses awhile for reflection,
And bolts at top pace in the other direction;
Goes down to the town, and soon finds he's in luck,
For a buyer turns up, and the bargain is struck.
Impatient, his ill-gotten gains he then 'collars',
(I think the amount is about fifty dollars),
He 'shroffs' the whole sum,—'tis all right,—then he borrows
A purse, puts it up, and next drowns all his sorrows
In a cup of good *saké*,[3] and starts home half 'tight,'
Having promised delivery that very night;
And he quiets his scruples,—that is, if he's any,—
By the thought that he's turned a felicitous penny!

---

3. *Saké*,—a liquor brewed from rice, the national beverage of Japan.

'Tis a lonely moor
At the ev'ning hour,
   And the moon's behind a cloud,
And the shadows fall
Like a heavy pall,
   And the earth with darkness shroud;
Not a leaf is stirred,
Not a sound is heard
   Save the howl of a distant dog,
Or the croak so harsh,
From the noisome marsh,
   Of the ever wakeful frog!
You can scarce distinguish the faint outline
   Of yon rickety, ruin'd old Shintô shrine!

Yoichibei's hastening back to his home,
And wishes he'd reached it, I'm sure, for to roam
In such darkness as this cannot be over nice,—
Never mind, he'll be there,—so he thinks,—in a trice.
But the way it is long, and his legs they are old,
And the moor's heavy walking, the night it is cold;
He's close by the shrine, and, quite pleased at the sight,
Says,—" I'll rest for a moment, and just strike a light,
" And before going on to my supper of tripe
" Will solace my cares with a whiff of my pipe."

   His pipe being finished,
   His cares, too, diminished,
He thinks he'll proceed, but will first take a sight
Of his ill-gotten cash, to make sure it's all right;—
   But while holding his prize
   Close up to his eyes,

The better to view it, there comes a surprise !
From the shrine, which resembles an old rabbit hutch,
Forth darts a long arm, which the money does clutch !
    A noise,—a crash,—
    A stunning smash,—
A fearful form,—and a sword-blade's flash,—
And a robber has settled Yoichibei's ' hash ! '
As this "knight of the road" proves to be a hard hitter,
And the blow's what the Japanese term a 'pear splitter,'
(That's full on the crown), the old woodman goes down,
With a shriek that is probably heard in the town !

The robber's a jovial man in his way,
He looks on such accidents merely as play ;
He counts up the money,—a satisfied smile
Illumines his villanous features the while ;
    When, just in front,
    Is heard the grunt
Of a boar that is fleeing away from a hunter, who follows with shouts,—this the robber does scare,
The purse he lets fall, and runs off like a hare.
    Just then the moonlight
    Gives the hunter a sight
Of his prey (as he thinks)—he's not up to it quite,
But he'll risk a long shot,—so, with sportsmanly vigour,
Claps his gun to his shoulder, and straight pulls the trigger ;
The boar goes off scatheless, but oh ! and alack !
The shot hits the highwayman plump in the back !

DEATH OF YOICHIBEI.

The hunter—'tis Hayano—quickens his pace,
" I've got him, that's certain ; about here's the place,"—
So he gropes in the dark, like a man full of toddy,
And at last stumbles over Yoichibei's body.
" Hurrah ! here's the boar ! "—and he draws, in a
    crack,
From his belt a stout cudgel, with which he gives
    whack
    Upon whack
    On the back
Of his parent defunct, on his sides, on his head,
Till he's certain the beast, as he thinks it, is dead ;
Never dreaming—(how should he ?—the corpse he
    ne'er saw)—
That he's only been thrashing his father-in-law !
A rope he produces, intending to bind
His prey on his back,—he stoops,—what does he find ?
Oh, horror !—a moonbeam shines forth,—pale and
    wan
He beholds, staring upwards, the face of a *man !*
    Straightway all his joy
    Turns to *'otototoi*,
(That's a word, reader, known to the youngest school-
    boy ;
But if you by chance have forgotten your Greek,
To enlighten your ignorance here I will speak ;—
Victor Hugo explains it, then, dearest *lecteur*,
As a term that *parfaitement exprime la douleur).*

    Over Hayano's face
    Comes an awful grimace,
        As he thinks of the deed he has done ;

Though not truly to blame,
He's so covered with shame
    That he once again charges his gun;
Then the muzzle he points
To the place where the joints
    Of his neck fasten on to his breast,
Puts it well in position,
With sighs of contrition,
    And then,—(though it must be confessed
With a hand somewhat shaky)—he finally fires,
Tumbles flat on his back like a log, and—expires?—
No such thing, reader, somehow the aim proves
    untrue,
And our hero soon rises without more ado.
After all, it's sheer folly, he thinks, thus to die,—it
's all madness,—he will not a second time try it!
After all, matters possibly might have been worse;
And just here his hand happens to fall on the purse.
This settles the question,—the money he takes,
And starts for his home ' in a couple of shakes!'
Quite without an idea of the dreadful reality,
Knowing nought of the poor, old deceased's per-
    sonality.

But as all this is passing, the night has grown late,
And the women at home in the cottage await,
    With hearts somewhat anxious, their husbands'
        return;
Their stomachs are empty, they're longing to learn
What the chances of food are, or how they shall
    sup,
When a knock at the door quickly rouses them up;—

"Yoichibei!"—"Hayano!"—loud they exclaim,—
The door they fling open,—what's this?—by the flame
Of the fire on the hearth they see, leading the van,
Two ugly old hags and an ugly old man;
In the rear are some coolies who carry a chair,
And who curse with loud voices the cold midnight air.
The ugly old trio advance, and they say—
"We've come for the damsel we purchased to-day!"

Just fancy the look Mrs. Hayano wears!
She can't make it out, so she stands and she stares;
While Yoichibei's wife, who of course "twigs" the
    joke,
Invites them to enter,—they laughingly poke
One another's lean ribs, and then sit down and smoke.
    Their errand's explained,
    They can't be detained,
Their home in the town must at once be regained;
"So give us the damsel, old lady,—be quick;
"The cash has been paid,—look alive, there's a
    brick!"
    Now Mrs. H. is in deadly fear,
      And ghastly is her look,
    As she views those hags with looks so drear,
    As she watches that old man's ugly sneer,
    As she marks her mother's cunning leer,
      And the memorandum-book
In which is noted the price they've paid
For herself,—poor timid, helpless maid!
'Tis *shikata ga nai*,—(that's the way that the Japs.
Say, "No help for it")—so she just packs up her
    traps;

  And gets into the chair,
   Which the coolies then bear
Aloft on their shoulders,—no prospect is there
Of escaping her fate, howsoe'er she may try,
So she sits herself down for a hearty good cry!

The ugliest hag stays behind for awhile,
Now chatting, now smoking, now helping to pile
On the fire some fresh brushwood,—when, sudden, a
   knock
At the door gives the pair a perceptible shock!
The hag she turns white, Mrs. Y. she turns blue,
As Hayano enters without more ado.—
" Mrs. Y.!—I've been lucky ; some dollars I've got,
" That will help us to buy something nice for the pot ;
" Never mind how I earned them,—they'll just save
   our life—
" But, hallo!—by the way, what's become of my wife ?"

You can fancy the tumult to which this gives rise,—
The agonised look in the fond husband's eyes,—
Mrs. Y.'s terror-stricken and cringing servility,—
The beetle-browed hag's oaths and open scurrility!
Till Hayano flings down the purse with a smack,
And roundly exclaims that he'll soon buy her back—
" What's the 'damage,' you crone?—Fifty dollars?—
   that's nice ;
" Here's th' identical sum ;—fetch her back in a trice!"
   With threats and with frown
   He stalks up and down,
His mother-in-law hides her face in her gown ;
But the hag, on her knees at the side of the fire,

Examines the purse, and then turns to inquire
As to where he obtained it,—" it's very much like
" A purse of my own ;"—here a thought seems to strike
Poor Hayano's mind,—but again at the door
Comes a rap (that's the third one) ;—he crosses the floor,
And opens the portal,—sees three of his neighbours,
Who tell that, whilst bound to their homes from their labours,
They happened to pass o'er the moor, and there found
Yoichibei's corpse lying stiff on the ground.
 Before their eyes
 The body lies,
The widow howls, and moans, and cries ;
Not liking to witness such sad tribulation,
The neighbours troop off in some slight consternation.

 With gleaming eyes
 The hag does rise,
And produces a *second* purse,—just the same size.
Shape, and hue as the one which our hero had brought,
That he starts at the sight like a person distraught.
 " Look here, Mrs. Y. !"
 She exclaims, with a cry
That makes Hayano jump, tho' he scarce can tell why ;
" Look here !—these two purses belong both to *me* ;
" One I lent to your husband this morning, when he
" To sell yonder damsel to us did agree !
 " The murder, I say,
 " Is plain as the day.
" This ruffian met your old man on the way

"To your house, struck him down, and the money did
    rob :—
("Poor dear! what a terrible crack on his nob!)—
   "These purses, I swear,
   "Well his treason declare ;
"The murdered lies here, and the murderer's *there* !"
And she points to our hero, who horror-struck stands,
As the hag grasps his arm with her long skinny
    hands :—
   His face assumes an ashen hue,
     His parchèd lips are dry ;
   The women seize him at the view,
     And raise a hue and cry ;
   The hag has grabbed him from behind,
     The widow from before,—
   They rate him first with words unkind,
     Then hurl him to the floor,
And with some handy faggot-sticks belabour him full
    sore !

Against the pair he nought can do, save loudly curse
    his fate,
While blows descend amain upon his back, and sides,
    and pate ;
Till, almost dead, with aching head, he's in a corner
    thrown ;—
He opes his eyes, and strives to rise, and thus he
    makes his moan ;—
"Alas! that I, a *samurai*[4] of noble house and fame,
"Should thus so undeservedly have earned a felon's
    name !

---
4. Samurai,—a man of the military class, entitled to carry two swords.

SUICIDE OF KAMPEI.

"In very truth,
"No crime, in sooth,
   "Can at my door be laid,
"Though facts may seem,
"You rightly deem,
   "To prove my wicked trade.
"I never slew Yoichibei intentionally, though
"I own my bullet wrought his death,—but then, I'd
   have you know
"I aimed but at a flying boar;—alas! what dire
   mischance
"Could e'er have caused the ball from off some tree
   aside to glance,
"And wound my dear old *père*-in-law!—Enough, no
   more say I,—
"Though Hayano dishonored live, he can with honor
   die,
"I'll make my exit as becomes a gentle *samurai!*"

   His dirk he grips,
   His mantle strips,
      Then, with a fixèd smile,
   The blade he draws,—
   A moment's pause,—
      He looks at it awhile,
Examines it from end to end,—makes up his mind,—
   and then,
He sheathes the steel, up to the hilt, in his own
   abdomen!

Most dramatists like, at the end of a play,
To bring on the stage the whole glitt'ring array

  Of the actors ;—this rule,
   In the Japanese school,
   Is the same, without doubt,
   For it here comes about
Mrs. Hayano suddenly makes her appearance,—
(Let's hope from her captors she's got a full clear-
    ance) ;—
But alas! what a sight for her conjugal eyes!
   On the floor,
   In his gore,
   With a wound deep and sore,
Her heart's-beloved Hayano weltering lies!
Such a climax of evils would worry a saint,
So she sinks on the ground, and goes off in a faint!

Next enter two gentlemen, bravely attired,
Tho' their garments are travel-stained, smirched, and
   bemired ;
   By the crest
   On their breast
   It may plainly be guessed
They're two of the vassals who had to disperse
When gallant lord Asano met his reverse.
Poor Hayano strives to sit upright,
And welcomes the pair with words polite :
They tell how their chieftain's untimely doom
Has cast on his vassals a moody gloom,
Any how they've resolved to have the head
Of the man by whose means their lord is dead ;
Though many have sworn to assist the feat,
The number, they say, is not yet complete,—
" One name on the muster-roll yet we require,

"And Hayano Kampei's the man we desire!"
Poor Kampei groans,—he's growing pale,—
He feebly falters forth his tale;
The guests perceive his altered glance,
They mourn his fate;—and then, by chance,
    They both draw near
    The dead man's bier;
What's this?—how's that?—what have we here?
    They roll their eyes
    In wild surprise,
Then point to the spot where the body lies;—
They seize on the shroud—aside they pull it—
The wound's from a *sword-blade*, not a *bullet*!
'Tis proved that he's innocent!—oh what a ' muff'
To go and destroy himself while in·a huff,
When a casual glance would have proved the clear
    fact
That Yoichibei's death was some other man's act!
And, to clear up the myst'ry, there now rushes in
A messenger, breathless, and wet to the skin
(For it's raining in torrents), who shouts from the door
That the corpse of the highwayman's found on the
    moor;—
He's a bandit who'd long robbed, remorseless and
    cruel,
And the folks all rejoice he's at last " got his gruel;"—
The man himself dances,—his joy knows no lack
Since a monster like this has been *shot through the back!*

But Hayano's life flickers low in its socket,
When the gentlemen turn, and produce from a pocket
The roll of the names of those vassals so true,

And one says, with a smile,—" Mr. Hayano, you
" By your soldier-like bearing have shown yourself fit
" To be classed with the rest of us,—just wait a bit,—
" Quick, a pen there!—I'll here add your name at the
    heel
" Of the list, and will trouble you now for your seal!"
See, the dying man drags himself over the floor,
And he puts for his seal some few drops of his gore,—
Then suddenly sinks, and, with fast-closing eyes,
Falls forward,[5] and so like a gentleman dies!

    What was done, what was said,
      When poor Kampei was dead,—
If the widow e'er got the facts right in her head,—
Are matters not mentioned in subsequent hist'ry,
In fact, I believe that they still are a myst'ry;
Such being the case, then,—since nobody knows 'em,
I'll leave you, kind reader, yourself to suppose 'em!

MORAL.

I.

If you're thinking of suicide, pray do not flurry;
For a thing is ne'er done *well* that's done in a hurry!

II.

    When out hunting, beware
      Of your gun, and take care
That you don't yourself fall into some ugly snare;

---

5. This was held to be the proper mode in which a person committing *hara-kiri* should sink to the ground. To facilitate falling in this posture, the long sleeves of the outer garment (the upper part of which was thrown off from the shoulders) were usually tucked tightly under the knees, as the man knelt, or rather squatted, in Japanese style.

And mind you don't murder, where'er you may be,
A *boar* that's not spelt with an *a* but an *e*!

III.

Last of all,—should you find, when your pockets are
    empty,
A slave-market close by, and handy, and tempty,
Remember Yoichibei's fate,—what it tells is,
Don't sell your own daughter,—sell somebody else's!

THE FATAL ERROR.

THE "Kaga-Sôdô," the drama from which the following fragment is taken, is, like the "Chiushin-gura," founded on fact. The intrigues therein related are supposed to convey some idea of those that actually occurred in the middle of the 17th century at the Castle-town of Kanazawa, the seat of the Maëda family who were lords of the rich province of Kaga in which that town is situated. The particular scenes described in the verses are no doubt highly colored, and it is but fair to state that the tale of the "Kaga-Sôdô," as represented on the stage, differs considerably from the real occurrences as recorded in Japanese historical annals. Be that as it may, the drama is an exceedingly popular one; and although, as a whole, it is perhaps slightly tedious, those particular scenes which relate to the exciting adventures of one of the retainers of the lord of Kaga may possibly prove of some interest. We leave our friends to judge for themselves.

he Fatal Error;

A Fragment from the Japanese Play of "Kaga Sódó" ("The Disturbance in Kaga"), as Performed at the Saruwaka-machi Theatre, Asakusa, Tokio.

WITH a sorrowful face, and a mystified frown,
  The Councillor wandereth up and adown;
 There's a glance in his eye
 That is plainly *shimpai*,[1]
And the badge on his mantle is pulled all awry;
His chin is unshaven; on top of his pate
His queue draggles down in a sad dirty state;
 In the broad girdle laced
 Round his corpulent waist
Are his swords in a fashion most slovenly placed,
With the short one *inside*, which, a child could descry,
Is a mode quite unworthy a true *samurai*;
His mien is dejected; o'ercome by his woe,
He looks more like a guy than a gallant *karó!*[2]
And, in view of these symptoms, to think you're inclin'd
That a something doth trouble the Councillor's mind.

---

1. *Shimpai,*—troubled, concerned.
2. *Karó,*—literally "elder," a Councillor of a daimió. The office was hereditary, and some nobles had several Councillors.

Yes, you're right, gentle reader; he cannot refuse
To admit that he's down with a fit of the blues;
    And just here, I would pray
    You'll permit me to say
That the question of *colour*'s quite strange in its way;
Thus, a man owns he's *blue*, but I've never yet seen
Any person so bold as confess himself *green!*—
'To return to our muttons' from this slight digression,
I'll tell you the cause of our worthy's depression:
If a man e'er had 'blues,' 'tis the case with our friend,
And, of course, there's a lady to blame in the end!

    "Oh! alas for the day,"
    Doth the Councillor say,
"When our late Kashiu Sama the good passed away!
"While he lived, peace and plenty prevailed in our
    land,
"And the peasants all blessed his beneficent hand;
"*Then* officials were honest, *then* taxes were light,
"*Then* our harvests were rich, and our prospects were
    bright,
"And a tub of good *saké* was broached ev'ry night!
"And we fancied—poor fools!—'twould be always the
    same,
"As we bragged of our clan and our *daimió*'s fame:
    "But, alas and alack!
    "One fine day an attack
"Of sore sickness prostrated our lord on his back;
"Some they swore it was *kak'ke*,[3] some vowed 'twas
    from drink,

---

3. *Kak'ké*,—a disease common in Japan, marked by paralytic and dropsical symptoms.

" They were all of them wrong,—for my own part,
　　　I think
" Any fool could have seen with but half of an eye,
" That the time had arrived for his lordship to die;
" His last hour was at hand, he perceived without
　　　telling,
" So at once set in order his household and dwelling;
" He looked out for his heir a most charming young
　　　wife,
" And then, greatly lamented, departed this life;
" Full of years and of honours, he died without pain,
" And was buried,—and then, there commenced a new
　　　reign;
" For his son (would that sad date could pass by un-
　　　heeded!)
" To his lands, titles, cash-box, and castle succeeded.

　　" Some few months passed away,
　　" And the Lady O Tei
" O'er our young chief's affections retained her first
　　　sway;
" And so gentle, so kind, so devoted was she,
" That of all the retainers no man could foresee
" That the Lord and his Lady would e'er disagree.
" Yet, ere long,—how it happened I'm sure I can't
　　　tell,—
" The gay youth 'gainst her counsels began to rebel,—
" Paid attentions, in fact, to a frail singing girl,
" Who ensnared his weak heart, set his brain in a
　　　whirl,
" And so stole his affections completely away
" From the wife of his bosom, poor Lady O Tei!

" Till at last the enchantress, without more ado,
" Made our lord bring her home as his wife *Number
 Two!!*

 " Oh! ne'er can I forget that morn,
 " The darkest day that e'er did dawn,
  " That viewed our chieftain's fall!
 " When, faithless to his loving spouse,
 " Forgetful of his plighted vows,
  " He sank in folly's thrall!
 " Oh! would he ne'er had known the wile
 " Of wanton Hidé's laughing smile,
  " Or seen her witching eye!
 " Far better 'twere that, hushed his breath,
 " And stilled his heart by friendly death,
  " He in the grave should lie!
" Yet the Lady O Hidé, I'll frankly concede,
" Is a damsel of marvellous beauty,—indeed,
" There's a weird, supernatural loveliness glows
" From the crown of her head to the tips of her toes!
" E'en when I, an old man, first encountered her
  glance,
" I could feel my poor heart give a palpable dance;
" While the blood in my veins coursed with feverish
  heat,
  " Till I hardly could well
  " Have attempted to tell
" If I stood, at the time, on my head or my feet!
" Nay, I scarce think she's human: for ne'er have I
  seen
" Any maiden of parentage mortal whose mien
" Was at once so majestic, enchanting, alluring!

("I'm convinced she's a demon; the thing's past
     enduring!)
" Then that smile so bewitching, those luminous eyes!
(" Oh! I'll swear she's a badger or fox [4] in disguise!)
     " Yet,—to think that that form,
     " Which an iceberg might warm,
" Should be that of a devil!—My eyes! what a storm
" Would have broke on my foolish, devoted old head,
" If so dire a suspicion in public I'd said!
" Yet the thing's past a doubt, from that sad, fatal
     day
" Our whole *matsurigoto* [5] has gone to decay;
" While our hapless young lord by th' enchantress
     will linger;
(" She can turn him with ease round her lily-white
     finger!)
" And, in view of these facts, and of signs not a few
" That dire mischief is brewing, what *am* I to do?
     " For the peasants all say,
     " In a gloomy, stern way,
" That they *won't* find the taxes they're ordered to pay;
" I'm afraid of some *ikki*, [6] I tremble with dread,
" And I curse the enchantress,—*I would she were
     dead!*"
     Here the puzzled *karō*,
     With a face full of woe,
Shakes his head, blows his nose, and declares it's
     'no go,'

---

4. Alluding to popular Japanese superstitions. Foxes and badgers are credited, in Japanese legends, with possessing the power of assuming at will the likeness of human beings.

5. *Matsurigoto*,—government administration.

6. *Ikki*,—agrarian riot.

Gives it up, and confesses, while heaving a sigh,
'Tis a regular case of *shikata ga nai*⁷ !
From behind the low hedge in the Councillor's rear,
With a loud rustling noise, see ! a form doth appear ;
And this form, as you yet more attentively scan,
The proportions assumes of a handsome young man.
    The *karô*, at the sound,
    Gives a start,—with a bound
The youth springs o'er the hedge, quickly glances
    around
To the right and the left,—not a soul's in the street—
So he sinks on his knees at the Councillor's feet !

" Hallo !—Kwansuké !—you rascal, how dare you come
    here ?
" Why, I thought I dismissed you my service last
    year !"—
" Oh ! I pray, good my lord, you'll vouchsafe to give
    ear,
    " And to list to my tale,
    " For I'm sure I shan't fail
" To explain my past conduct ;"—his master turns
    pale ;
" Only fancy," thinks he, " what a dreadful mishap
" If my threats should have chanced to be heard by
    this chap !
" I'll just hark to his tale, without anger or scoff,
" And, that done, I've no doubt I can soon ' bluff him
    off.' "
So the Councillor here, as old Horace would tell us,
" *Ut iniquæ* (that means ' stubborn ') *mentis asellus*,

---

7. " No help for it ! "

"*Demittit auriculas*" (that phrase can't hurt you)
And, in fact, of ' necessity dire ' makes a virtue ;
His retainer looks up with an air of combined
Joy and fear, clears his throat, and thus eases his
    mind :—
    " Words alone
    " Can't atone,
       " I most freely will own,
" For my past misdemeanors ;—my faults I bemoan,
" And I would that whilst I in your household did stay
" More befitting behaviour I'd tried to display ;
    " For I'm fully aware
    " That my conduct while there
" Was by no means *en règle*, nor yet on the square.
" I disturbed the whole place with my riot and noise,
" For my fault was, in short, I was ' one of the boys ;'
" And no matter what mischief the youngsters might
    brew,
" I was safe to be found at the head of the crew ;
" There was no one so apt at concocting a hoax,
" Or at starting a ' sell,' or low practical jokes ;
    " I'd dress up, for a lark,
    " When it chanced to be dark,
" In a sheet, like a ghost, promenading the park,
" When I'd frighten the waiting maids out of their
    wits,
" And once drove the fat cook pretty nigh into fits ;
" Till at last to yourself I once offered some ' slack,'
" For which you, most deservedly, gave me the sack !
" Thus dismissed in disgrace, I continued to roam,
" Cut by all my old chums, without shelter or home ;
" Till at last I encountered a kindly old man

"Who had known me in youth,
"And who promised in truth
"To befriend me if I'd begin new;—I began!
"I took service with him, and I've worked in his store,
("He's a dealer in dry goods) this twelvemonth and more;
"But I burn
"To return
"From this peddling concern
"To the life of a gentleman, once more to learn
"How to wield with precision the lance and the blade,
"In the stead of the cloth-yard that's used 'in the trade.'
"Oh! forgive me, kind master, forgive and forget
"All my former misdeeds, and I'll prove to you yet
"That your gracious beneficence largely can tend
"To assist me my reprobate ways to amend!"

"Well, well," says his *ci-devant* master, "'tis true
"That I always had, Kwansuké, a liking for you;
"That your past life was wrong, there can be no denial,
"Yet I'll not refuse once more to give you a trial:
"As I don't like to jump on a man when he's down,
"I'll assist you to try and achieve some renown.
"To ensure true success there is nought, I've oft felt,
"Like red gold in the purse, and sharp steel at the belt;
"You've just spoken of wielding the blade and the lance,—

THE COUNCILLOR AND KWANSUKE.

" Take this dirk, then, and purse,—these will give you
    a chance
" To distinguish yourself by some valorous deed,
" By some gallant *tegara*,[8] —and then, as the meed
    " Of your vict'ry, I'd fain
    " Treat the past with disdain,
" And install you, thus proved, in my service again."

    " Thanks! noble sir!" doth Kwansuké cry,
      " For this thy kind goodwill;
    " I'll do some deed of merit high,
      " To prove I'm worthy still;
    " For Kwansuké's breast is bold and leal,
      " Of that be not afraid;
    " His heart is true as the burnished steel
      " Of a Masamuné blade!"[9]
With a low genuflection, the gifts he doth seize,
Holds them up to his forehead, then sinks on his
    knees,
And his face to the paving stones flatly doth squeeze,
With that sibilant noise which, as some writers men-
    tion,
' Doth an attitude show of respectful attention!'
The Councillor smiles, bids his servant be brave,
Turns away, and with features once more set and
    grave,
Passes in through the gateway that stands on his
    right,
And the large heavy doors shut him out from our sight.

---

8. Tegara,—act of merit, doughty deed.
9. Masamuné,—one of the most famous swordsmiths of Japan, lived from 1264 to 1343 A.D. It is, in Japanese literature, a common metaphor to compare a loyal heart to a trusty sword-blade.

Kwansuké lies for a moment, and then, with a bound
Like a harlequin, rises again from the ground.
First he pauses, and drops a salt tear at the view
Of the strong massive portal he dare not pass through;
(Like the Peri who, Thomas Moore's tale doth relate,
Stood in sorrow and wept near the Paradise Gate;)
    Next, the purse he unties,
    And evinces surprise
At the rich store of *nibu*[10] that greets his glad eyes,
Rolls it up as before, and conceals it beneath
The wide folds of his dress; then he draws from its
    sheath
The bright sword that's to carve him a fortune anew,
And stands almost entranced as the steel meets his
    view:
" What a beautiful weapon! how perfectly made!
" And what exquisite fittings! how trenchant a blade!
" And see here, on the sheath, too, quite plain to
    behold,
" The good Councillor's badge worked in lacquer and
    gold!
" Good! this sword shall remind me, where'er I may
    go,
" Of the grand debt that I to my master now owe:
" If he'd only a foe! then to prove my sincerity
" I'd be down on the chap with most *killing* asperity!
" Yet, just hold for a moment,—yes, didn't he say
" That the Lady O Hidé had caused his dismay?
    " And he furthermore said
    " That he 'would she were dead,'
" And invoked sundry curses to fall on her head:

---

10. Gold pieces, worth about fifty cents each.

"She's 'ensnared our young Lord'?—then my duty
    is plain;
"I'll take pretty good care she don't do so again,
"For in view of the fact that her conduct is *sich*,"
(Rhyme demands that word, reader,) "*I'll 'go for'*
    the witch!"

Having made up his mind, and determined his victim,
He at once flies away as though Benkei [11] had kick'd
    him!

  The scene is changed. A lordly hall
   Before our eyes is laid;
  On post and ceiling, beam and wall,
   Are paintings rare portrayed;
  Here vase of price, there silken shawl,
   Is carelessly displayed;
And gilded badges plain declare,
'Tis Kashiu Sama's castle fair.

  Lovely ladies, gay and bright,
  Pass in groups before our sight;
  Dainty maidens, tall and slim,
  Fair of face, and lithe of limb;
  There, the fairest 'midst the throng,
  Witching Hidé moves along;
  Far outshines each rival, far
  As the comet shames the star,
  As the snow-white *sagi* [12] shows
  'Midst a flock of sable crows!

---

11. Benkei,—the Hercules of Japan. He lived in the latter half of the 12th century.
12. Sagi,—the white 'paddy-bird'; allusion is here made to a Japanese proverb.

   Blind to all, on her we gaze;
   Listen, while I sing her praise.
Imprimis, a nose, which (though perfect, *I*'d say),
Some *might* deem a trifle too much *retroussé;*
Next, a sweet dimpled chin, and two cherry-red lips,
With a smile that e'en Venus's own might eclipse;—
   But my Muse says, " Enough !"
   And turns off in a huff;
Of description she thinks you have quite *quantum suff.;*
   And, thus hearing her rail,
   All my energies fail :—
As to paint the fair damsel mere words can't avail,
I'll give up the hard task, and go on with my tale;
Leaving each of my readers to fill in the rest
As to him (or to *her)* may appear to be best!
   Yet I own I'm inclin'd
    First to speak out my mind,
   Thus,—I wouldn't give much for the man
    Who can not in his heartstrings a tender spot find
    For the daughters of lovely Japan!
   And this one fact I'll tell my Muse,
    Nor heed her angry tone,—
   Stood *I* in Kashiu Sama's shoes,
    I'd do as *he* has done !

To resume then ;—'tis winter, the sky's dull and drear
As is mostly the case at this season of year;
   And foot-deep on the ground
   Lies the snow all around
The proud castle, so thick that it deadens the sound
Of the peasant's slow footsteps, as plodding he goes
Down the road to the town, with his fingers and toes

Quite benumbed, while long icicles hang from his nose!
    (And just here I may say
    It's quite strange, by the way,
How the Japanese love snowy scenes to portray
On those long *kakémono* [13] you notice each day;
If you order "a winter scene," gladly I'll lay
Ten to one—that's long odds, but there's 'nary'
    mistake in it—
That they paint you a snow-storm, and mandarin-
    drake in it!)

    To-day fair Hidé fain would go
      To view the landscape o'er,
    Clothed in its garb of spotless snow;
      Her train is at the door,
    And Lady Hidé's palanquin
      Too long has "stopped the way,"
    And yet she lingers still within;
      What makes my lady stay?
The reason, kind reader, I'll tell you full soon,
Her Ladyship's fainted, gone off in a swoon!—
What a shocking catastrophe! in rush her maids.
Bearing hartshorn, burnt feathers, and sundry more
    aids
To restore animation; her system is strong,
And she 'comes to' completely before very long.
Ah! Lady O Hidé! was't purposely done?
Was that sickness a *feint* in more senses than one?
Were you warned to beware, by some merciful dream,
Of yon dark form awaiting you down by the stream?

---

13. *Kakémono*,—long hanging scrolls, fitted with rollers at the top and foot, used to decorate the walls of a room.

True or false, I can't say,
Be that all as it may,
The fact stands,—'twas the death-knell of Lady O Tei!
For, on hearing the tumult, that much-injured dame
Rushes forth, her eyes gleaming with jealousy's flame;
"Ha! gone off in a faint?" mutters she,—"let her stay!
"And, as *she* can't go out, I suppose that *I* may;
"'Tis a sin to keep coolies thus waiting all day."
With a glance at her rival stretch'd prone on the floor,
She steps into the litter, and starts from the door.

'Tis a wintry day,
And the sun's last ray
  O'er the landscape pure and white
Is sinking slow,
And the sparkling snow
  Is tinged with its golden light;
And the piercing blast
Sends driving past
  The snow in feath'ry flake,
Where the willows rear
Their forms so drear
  Beside the frozen lake;
And the trees' are bare,
Through the chill, bleak air
  Is the curlew's whistle heard,—
The curlew wild,
By Bret Harte styled
  "That melancholy bird!"—
(But, indeed, the poor curlew has plenty of reason
To be rather down-hearted at such a bad season;

For, in fact, 'tis enough to depress any *man*,
To be snow-bound, by night, on a moor in Japan!)

Yet there's *one* man, at least, who cares nought for
    the snow;
On his hands and his knees he creeps 'stealthily slow,'
As if dreading detection, to where on the bank
Of the stream stands a patch of reeds, slimy and dank;
Soon their shelter he gains, and there crouches full
    low,
While his foot-prints are hid by the thick-falling snow;
    There he silently lies,
    Ever straining his eyes
Towards the height where the castle's tall battlements
    rise
In a huge, looming mass 'fore the darkening skies.
    Is he stalking a deer?
    Does he strive to get near
To the wary wild goose, in the hope of a shot?
No; I'm sure I can boldly affirm he does *not;*
No; he's bound, to *my* eyes, on no errand so tame,
For his look makes me fancy he seeks nobler game;
And I think, with *one* stroke (if the truth must be
    told)
He'll have killed rather more than a game-bag can
    hold!
    See him rise once again—
    For a moment remain
Fix'd and stern—then prostrate himself flat on the
    plain!
He has sighted his prey!—hark! a *click*—then a
    pause—

Then a dull, sliding sound—we can *feel* that he draws
From its scabbard the hunting-knife, soon to be dyed
In the blood of his quarry!—he turns to one side,—
With a back-handed twitch flings the sheath on the
    snow,—
But reveals, while so doing, a face that we know!
It is Kwansuké!—depend on't, the deed will be done,
For he's plainly gone in for 'the whole hog or none!'
See! from out the dark shadows obscuring the plain,
With a slow, steady tramp comes the nobleman's train;
All so silent, so solemn, you'd think that you view
Not a body of men, but some weird spectral crew!
Through their ranks not a sound, not a whisper is
    breathed.
Each retainer's sword-handle's in oil-paper sheathed;
    As a fence 'gainst the storm,
    And to keep himself warm,
In a rain-coat each man has envelop'd his form;
On their feet thick straw sandals are carefully laced,
And their heads with large round hats of bamboo are
    graced;
Till, in fact, each stout vassal appears to our eyes
Like an overgrown mushroom of marvellous size!
In the midst, on their shoulders, six coolies uphold
The gay litter, all deck'd with blue velvet and gold,—
The gay litter, in short, of the Lady O Tei;
And behind come more coolies to act as relay;
While the lance and the halberd, the plume and the
    spear,
All around their fair mistress her vassals uprear;
Such the emblems of rank which you always might see
Round a Japanese noble of lofty degree.

THE ATTACK ON THE TRAIN.

Slowly marches the train,—some fatality leads
It direct towards that ill-omen'd dark patch of reeds;
In a moment—so swift that it plainly appals
E'en the boldest among them—the thunderbolt falls!

    Hark to the agonizing cries,
    The shrieks of pain that loudly rise!
    The work of death young Kwansuké plies
      Amidst his startled foes!
    These on their comrades wildly call,
    Those turn to fight,—'tis useless all—
    Man after man they reel and fall
      Beneath his deadly blows!
At the onset the vassals are scared with dismay,
As with strength superhuman he forces his way
    Towards the litter,—but then
    They all rally like men;
And just here, reader kind, if I'd only the pen
Of the 'Press Correspondents' who're granted facilities
For observing those sad Russo-Turkish hostilities,
(It would seem as the war had engross'd their whole
    heart in it),
    I'd describe to you now
    Such a rattling good row
As would make you quite anxious yourself to take part
    in it!
For at once I'd narrate, without pause or ahem,
How they lay on to him, and he 'lams' into them—
How their hats and their cloaks are flung quickly
    aside,—
How they tug at their sword-hilts, in oil-paper tied,
(Far too tightly, alas!)—how they hack and they hew

At th' assailant, who hacks, cuts, and thrusts at them too,
Till the dead and the wounded lie scatter'd around,
While their life-blood empurples the snow on the ground!
At such writing, however, I'm not quite *au fait*,
So will merely describe the 'fag end' of the fray:
See! the last coolie drops, almost cleft to the chin,
And our hero's alongside the gay palanquin;
See! he tears down the blind, forces open the door—
Then a long, wild shriek rises—the tragedy's o'er!
Here I think with Sir Walter "'twere sorrow to tell"
The full tale of the sad "butcher-work that befel;"
So suffice it to mention that Lady O Tei
Will not trouble her hair-dresser much from to-day!

    With a furious shout,
    In a menacing rout,
(For, *at last*, ev'ry man has his *katana*[14] out)
Here the remnant of vassals come up at a run;
But too slow to catch Kwansuké!—his foul errand's done,
So he heads for the stream at the deuce of a pace,
Like an athlete who starts for a hundred yards' race;
Soon he reaches its brink, having 'dodged' all his foes,
Plunges in—and the dark waters over him close!

    Here I'll leave you to guess
    Both the shame and distress
Which the luckless retainers now plainly express,
As they gaze on their lady's corpse (wanting a head!)
And then reckon the list of their wounded and dead.

---

14. *Katana*,—the long Japanese sword, as opposed to the *wakizashi* or dirk.

They're o'ercome with emotion, fear-stricken and awed ;
What account can they render for this to their lord ?
They've abandoned their mistress, they've let her be
    slain,
And they feel explanations will prove but in vain ;
Then, their foe was but one single swordsman, and he,
To their rage and chagrin, has retreated scot-free !
Matters clearly have come to a desperate pass ;
So they raise up the litter (now lighter, alas !)
Than it was when they started at noontide to-day)
And, with sighs of dejection and looks of dismay,
To the dark-frowning castle they take their sad way ;
And I think, if I read their blank faces aright,
There'll be cases of *seppuku*[15] happen to-night !
Once again the scene changes :—we plainly descry
'Tis the opposite side of the river—our eye
Merely rests on a bank built to keep off the flood,
While beneath it strong timbers project from the mud.
Ah, look there ! from the water, all dripping and dank,
There emerges a form, which crawls up the steep bank !
'Tis the form of a *man*—but so dreadful a sight
That you'd almost believe him some foul river sprite !
In his mouth is a drawn sword,—and see ! just beneath,
From its long raven tresses fast clutch'd 'twixt his
    teeth,
With its features all writhed and distorted with dread
As when hewn from the trunk, hangs *a fresh-severed*
    head !
Look ! he reels and he staggers, he hardly can stand,
'Tis a wonder he's ever got safely to land ;

---

15. Soppuku,—the Japanese rendering of the sound of the two Chinese characters used in writing to denote the word *hara-kiri*, or suicide by disembowelment.

For, between his long swim, and his recent hard bout,
Mr. Kwansuké's undoubtedly wholly 'played out'!
Down he sinks on the ground—then he struggles to rise
On his knees—with his hand wipes the spray from his eyes—
Lastly, sits himself down to examine his prize.

I don't know if your skill, reader, e'er you've essayed
At a game that's called 'poker' (extensively played
In the 'States')—if you *have*, you've most probably seen
And remarked the queer change that comes o'er a man's mien,
When he's drawn a fifth card which is not worth a rush,
And which leaves him with what's styled 'a darn'd busted flush'!
Just conceive, now, the look that his face would display
If a pool of a million gold dollars then lay
On the table before him,—next try, if you can,
To intensify *ten times* the look of that man ;—
Well, you've now got an inkling, from all I have said,
Of the glance of wild agony, horror, and dread
That comes o'er Kwansuké's face as he stares at the head!

Now I trust, for humanity's sake, that just here
There are none too hard-hearted to squeeze out a tear,
Yes, a salt tear of sympathy pure and unfeign'd,
O'er the 'crushing bad luck' that our hero's sustain'd!
    First, the poor fellow's lain
    Half the day on the plain,
At the cost of much sorrow and anguish and pain,

Sadly tortured with frost-bitten hands, ears, and feet,
And with nothing to drink, nor a morsel to eat;—
He's imperilled his life, too, in battle's fierce shock,
And his head shows the traces of thump and of knock
Dealt by Kaga's retainers who, void of compassion,
Have abused their advantage in barbarous fashion;—
Then he's, thirdly, been duck'd in the river so cold;—
And to find—after all—that he's only been '*sold*'!
That Dame Fortune, who loves such vagaries to play,
Having led him a dance, has then stoop'd to betray;
For she's mockingly thrown to poor Kwansuké, instead
Of the prize that he's hoped for, *a different head!*
'Tis enough to drive frantic the veriest saint!
And I won't try the task of attempting to paint
    His expression so black,
    As he hurls the head back
In the dark swollen river that rushes beneath:
Next he wraps up his sword (being *minus* its sheath)
In a blue cotton kerchief he draws from his breast,
And so leaves the sad scene with a visage depress'd;
While with deep lamentation he groans and he whines
O'er the thought of enduring such 'awful hard lines'!

Chang'd again is the scene:—Now before us there lies
A poor fisherman's hut of diminutive size—
    It is ev'ning,—and there
    Are a jovial pair—
This a man, that a damsel remarkably fair—
Who are just sitting down with a keen hungry air
    To their frugal repast;
    (They don't know 'tis the last
That as brother and sister together they'll share!)

Well, to cut matters short, I will here tell you plain
That this hut is the place where young Kwansuké has
    lain
Safely hid, since his fruitless attack on the train;
    And his sister so keen
    For his comfort has been,
As to share his long exile, and rule his *cuisine!*
How they ply their long chopsticks! How deftly the fish
And the *daikon*'s [16] transferred to their mouths from
    the dish!
How they go for their *saké!*—but ah! long before
They have ended their meal, comes a bang at the door,
And in walks an intruder, who startles them sore;—
(Like that Captain Miles Standish, unbidden who came
To the gay marriage-feast of his Puritan 'flame'!)
Down he flings his large hat, down his mantle does
    throw—
'Tis our hero's old master, the agèd *karô!*
With a kind salutation, he squats on the mat,
And, without more preamble, commences to chat.

    " On a night cold and drear,
    " In December last year,
" When returning from town, and when fast drawing
    near
" To the castle, my foot, 'neath the snow on the ground,
" Struck an object—I stooped, and this scabbard I
    found:"—
(He produces it)—" Fancy, again, my surprise,
" When the badge of my household thereon met my
    eyes!

---

16. *Daikon*,—the long Japanese radish.

THE COUNCILLOR'S VISIT.

THE FATAL ERROR.

" I remember'd well, Kwansuké, that lately to *you*
" I'd presented that scabbard, with sword in it too;
" How it came to be lost, how it chanced that it lay
" In the snow, I knew not—so continued my way.
 " At the castle that night
 " There was grief and affright ;
" And I learn'd, by degrees, the whole tale of the
  fight
" Which resulted, alas ! in the terrible death
" Of her ladyship—well, I of course held my breath
" As regards the sword-scabbard, nor stoop'd to betray
" My suspicions—but, Kwansuké, be candid, and say
" Was it *you* took the head off poor Lady O Tei ?"
Thus adjur'd, our young hero does plainly declare
All the facts, gentle reader, of which you're aware ;
How, conceal'd 'neath the hedge, he had clearly o'er-
  heard
Of the Councillor's tirade each separate word ;
How his blood it did boil, and his brain it did burn ;
How he thought to his patron he'd do a good turn,
By depriving the demon O Hidé of life ;
How he only found out at the *end* of the strife
That he'd fail'd in his scheme (to his infinite woe)
And ' instead of the pigeon had slaughter'd the crow !'
—Here, in proof of his tale, he produces the blade,
Which the sheath fits exactly, as though for it made.
—" I assure you, kind master, I frequently since
" Have endeavour'd to whisper the ear of our prince ;
" Being fully resolv'd, having made a ' clean breast,'
" And my fatal mistake having bravely confess'd,
" To commit *hara-kiri*, and die like a man,
" To proclaim my devotion to him and my clan !

" But no chance was forthcoming—Fate would not accord
" That poor Kwansuké should e'er meet with Kaga's proud lord ;
" Yet that object's attain'd, now I've met, sir, with you ;
" And there rests only *one* thing for Kwansuké to do !"
    Cries the Councillor, " Nay !
    " I beseech you to stay
" Your mad scheme, and just listen to what I shall say :
" You must know, then, our lord took it into his brain
" 'Twas through Hidé's foul plots that his lady was slain ;
" All the love that, while living, to her he'd denied
" Seem'd again to revive when he learn'd how she died ;
" He's a man of strong impulse, as doubtless you know,
" Quick he flung off the glamour that blinded him so,
" Gave O Hidé the sack, cast her off from his gate,
" And then turn'd his attention to matters of state ;
" What a weeding took place ! evil councillors went,
" Bad officials were all to the right-about sent—
" Bag and baggage he clear'd 'em out, every one,
" And has proved himself truly his good father's son !
" And this grand reformation, I take it, is due—
" Indirectly, of course—Mr. Kwansuké, to *you !*
" Pray don't think, then, of suicide—you're not betrayed—
" But re-enter my service ; your fortune is made !"

    With a sorrowful sigh,
    And a glance in his eye
That bespeaks resolution, does Kwansuké reply,—
" What ! you ask me to live—*me*, a true *samurai !*
" When the only resource that's yet left me's to die !

" You invite *me* to live—you beseech *me* to stay—
" When 'twas *I* struck the blow that slew Lady O Tei !
" I rejoice at the indirect fruits of my work ;
" For *myself*, though—stand by ! you *shall* yield me
    that dirk !"

All is o'er !—with his life's blood the ill-fated man
Has now sealed his devotion to chief and to clan !

MORAL.

I.

Married men ! I would first give a caution to you :—
Pay your wives that devotion that's rightly their due ;
And don't wander o' nights, nor be tempted to roam,
But as soon as it's sunset go soberly home !

II.

Married ladies ! if e'er you're inclined to be gay,
Think, oh ! think of the fate of poor Lady O Tei !

III.

Lovely damsels ! be warned by this drama so tragic :—
Learn that beauty ne'er needs the assistance of magic
To ensnare willing victims—no more potent wile
Do I know, than the charm of a fair maiden's smile !

IV.

Last of all, to young bachelors here I would speak :—
Don't be too fond of ' larking,' of joke, or of freak ;
Don't disturb honest folks when they're snugly abed,
And take care that you don't lose your *heart* or your
    head !

LADY KOKONOYÉ.

WHETHER the fair damsel who is the heroine of the following tale ever really existed is a question open to considerable doubt. That there was, however, once upon a time a nobleman named Amako, and that his retainers earned for themselves a high reputation for their devotion and fidelity to his service, is sufficiently proved by Japanese historical annals. But it is with the play and not with history that we have to deal; and as to the former a heroine is absolutely necessary, we can hardly do better than refrain from too close enquiry, contenting ourselves instead with what is told us about her in the drama alone.

Lady Kokonoye;

A Fragment from the Japanese play of "Amako Jiu-yu-shi" ("The Ten Valiant Retainers of Amako,") as Performed at the Haruki-machi Theatre, Hongô, Tôkiô, in January, 1878.

IN the province of Idzumo, west of Japan,
   'Midst as lovely a landscape as e'er you might scan,
Yoshihisa, the lord of an ample domain,
O'er the castle of Tomita blithely does reign;
Of the proud house of Amako chieftain is he,
And his fathers were nobles of lofty degree.
    Words would fail to narrate
    All his pomp and his state,
Or his riches and splendour in full to relate;
    So the news must suffice,
    That of ev'rything nice
That this world can afford he has got a good slice!
He's a wife, too, as fair as could possibly be,
Whom he loves as becomes a devoted *mari;*
He's an aged mamma (a most sanctified nun),
And one daughter—alas! he's not blessed with a son;
On behalf of that daughter I'd venture to claim
Your attention—my title will give you her name;

Stay, I'll just introduce you, in drawing-room style—
"Kokonoyé—my reader!"—(a curtsey, and smile).

  Fair Tokiwa's undying name
   Is writ on Hist'ry's page,
  Her matchless charms have left their fame
   To each succeeding age;
  She moved the Tyrant's heart of steel
   By simple loveliness;
  E'en Kiyomori's breast could feel
   For Beauty in distress:[1]
Yet, beside Kokonoyé, it's nought of affront
To assert that e'en Tokiwa's 'out of the hunt!'
Yes, my heroine's charming!—her figure so trim
As the willow tree's bough is as graceful and slim;
Her complexion's as white as is Fuji's hoar peak
'Neath the snows of midwinter—like damask her
   cheek—
  With a dear little nose,
  And two eyes black as sloes,
And a pair of ripe lips which, when parted, disclose
Pearly teeth—her fine eyebrows obliquely are set,
(In Japan that's a beauty)—her hair's dark as jet,
And is coiled in thick masses on top of her pate,
In a wonderful *chignon* as big as a plate:—
(There are *eight* styles of *chignon*, just here I may tell
My fair readers, as known to the Japanese *belle*).
Then, to heighten the beauty bestowed on the part
Of kind Nature, she's called in th' assistance of Art,

---

[1]. Alluding to an incident in Japanese history. Tokiwa, a young peasant-girl of surpassing beauty, was the concubine of Minamoto no Yoshitomo, and when the latter's family was almost annihilated in 1159 by Kiyomori, chief of the rival clan of Taira, she, by her loveliness, so moved the heart of the conqueror that he consented to spare the lives of her three sons.

LADY KOKONOYÉ.

LADY KOKONOYÉ.

For rice-powder to render more dazzlingly fair
Her face, hands, neck, and chin—cherry oil for her
    hair—
Just a *soupçon* of rouge to embellish her lip—
And a host of cosmetics my mem'ry that slip:—
To complete the fair picture of bright loveliness,
Add to all this the charm of her elegant dress;
    Satin, crape, and brocade
    Here contribute their aid
For the long flowing garments in which she's arrayed,
Which hang loose from her shoulders, in fanciful fold,
All embroidered with storks and plum-blossoms in
    gold;
Next, a broad velvet girdle encircles her waist,
Tied behind in a huge bow—her feet are encased
In small spotless white stockings, which timidly peep
From beneath her red *jupon*'s elaborate sweep;—
Add a hair-pin of tortoise-shell, dainty to see;
On her brow place a circlet of gilt filigree;—
There, in all the warm glow of her beauty, see shine
Kokonoyé, sole heiress of Amako's line!

    Now of course you'll agree,
    I feel certain, with me,
When a damsel's as lovely as lovely can be,
When her face is as fair as a face e'er has been,
And her figure's as graceful as ever was seen,
Above all, when the damsel's but 'sweet seventeen,'
And her young male acquaintances ardent and keen,
    In no matter what land,
    It to reason must stand
There'll be plenty of lovers to strive for her hand;—

When it's known, furthermore, that her father's
    possess'd
Of the wealth of this world, and has plainly express'd
His intention, whene'er his fair daughter shall wed,
To bestow more than blessings alone on her head,—
It may fairly be deemed that in trying to win
Her affections, *some* swains have an eye to the 'tin'!
—Well, from both of the causes I've mentioned above,
Crowds of suitors contend for my heroine's love;
Some are snared by *her* eyes—some (more numerous
    yet)
Font la cour aux beaux yeux de sa jolie cassette!
Shikanosuké's her choice;—no proud *daimió* he,
Hatamoto, or *kugé*[2] of lofty degree—
No, his *mibun*[3] is humble,—this favored young man
Is a vassal, in fact, of the Tomita clan:
Yet he's gentle by birth—by his lord trusted well—
And his feats and accomplishments scarce can I tell;
    He can beat any man
    Through the whole of Japan
At composing a verse to inscribe on a fan,—
(That's a great test of scholarship, doubtless you
    know)—
Then at sword-play, spear-practice, or drawing the bow,
Or at backing a steed, I may truthfully state,
He can match any youth of his own size and weight;
He has ne'er shunn'd a foe, nor sent friend to the
    wall—
He can drink like a *shôjô*[4]—at feast or in brawl

---

2. *Hatamoto,*—petty nobles of the old Shógunate: *kugé.*—Court nobles of Kióto (the Mikado's Court)—as opposed to the *daimió* or territorial nobles.

3. *Mibun,*—status, position in life.

4. *Shôjô,*—fabulous creatures, of human shape, with long red hair; said to be exceedingly fond of liquor.

He is equally ready his fortune to try—
And his comrades all vote him a true *samurai!*
He's a 'rising young man,' no one dares to dispute,
And the fair Kokonoyé has smiled on his suit!

    Full oft our lovers now explore
        The castle's farthest bounds,
    Together traverse o'er and o'er
        Its wooded pleasure-grounds;
    Oft ling'ring where some friendly bough
        Conceals from others' view,
    They breathe once more the tender vow,
        And plight their troth anew;
    And oft affect, while side by side
        Along the moat they stray,
    To watch the giant *koi*[5] glide
        Right leisurely away:—
Yes, it's all very fine for these two, I declare;
But just think of the *other* swains, left in despair!—
You may guess that some suitors were madly
    enraged
When they learned Kokonoyé was really 'engaged';
Some, they stormed and they raved, in a fume and a
    fret;
Others dubbed her a 'jilt,' and a 'heartless coquette;'
And some gloomily swore they'd commit suicide—
But 'tis needless to say *that* resource they ne'er tried,
For, ere long, Time had healed their sore-wounded
    affection,
And they turn'd their *amours* in some other direction!

---

5. Koi,—large fish, with which the ponds in Japanese pleasure-grounds are usually stocked. They often grow to an enormous size.

Terutsura alone (our lord's Councillor he)
To accept his rebuff could not,—*would* not agree ;
And he swore, which was coming it rather too
    strong,
He'd ' get even ' with young Shikanosuké ere long.

As ' the course of true love never smoothly did run,'
Here our fond couple's troubles have quickly begun,
And the *surgit amari*, commencement of woe,
Is all caused by the schemes of the wicked *karó ;*—
    First he cunningly tries,
    By a tissue of lies,
Shikanosuké to lower in Amako's eyes ;
And, that done, he contrives (this unprincipled man !)
That the youth shall be outlawed, and banished the
    clan ;
He himself bears the sentence, and mockingly gloats
O'er his victim's hard fate—Shikanosuké scarce notes
What he hears, but in voice unconcernèd does say,
" I expected as much—I will clear out to-day !"
—It would seem that our hero's already aware
Of his foe, and has managed his own counter-snare ;
Has committed, in fact, an *intentional* slip
(Which the Councillor takes as a negligent trip)
To ensure his dismissal, and leave himself free
To encompass the fall of his foeman, while *he*
O'er his fancied success is exulting with glee.—
Terutsura stalks out ;—there's a bang at the door,
Then a shuffle of feet,—some half-dozen or more
Of our hero's young chums rush excitedly in,
And pour forth their resentment with clamorous din—

" Shikanosuké, old man! we're in terrible grief:
" At the thought of your exile; 'tis past all belief
" That that rascally Councillor e'er should have dared
" Thus to do you a wrong—never mind, we're
        prepared
" Here to take our own lives, and thus plainly to
        show
" How indignant we feel 'gainst that scoundrel *karô!*"

    No further words they idly waste,
        But range them in a row;
    Down goes each mantle, doffed in haste,
        Their vests they open throw;
    Each steels his heart
    To act his part,
        Out comes each gleaming dirk;
    They only wait
    The signal, straight
        To start their awful work;—
    One moment more,
    'Twill all be o'er
        With each young heart so bold,—
    When, loud and stern, behind the door,
        A solemn voice cries " Hold!"
With a start ev'ry man turns around, and descries
An old priest, with bald pate and benevolent eyes!
(He's the priest of the temple, I here may explain,
'Neath whose roof Shikanosuké his lodging has ta'en.)
" Well, you *are* a nice lot," cries this worthy, " to try
" And defile my new mats in your hurry to die!
" Don't you think 'twould be better by far to remain
" In the land of the living?—What have you to gain

"By despatching yourselves?—Face your ills with a
    smile,
"And don't flee from bad luck in such cowardly
    style!"

    "Kind comrades all!"—our hero cries,
      "This monk the truth has said;
    "His counsel it is wondrous wise—
      "A thought comes in my head—
    "'Twere fitter, surely, that our *foe*,
      "Not *we*, our blows should feel;
    "Let's swear to teach yon proud *karô*
      "The temper of our steel!"

Suiting action to word, he takes paper and pen,
Writes a long form of oath, cons it over, and then
    Reads it out to the rest—
    There it's plainly express'd
That each man of the band will endeavour his best
To effect their false enemy's downfall and shame—
To this scroll, one by one, each affixes his name,
And, that done, with his knife gives a resolute score
To his left hand's fourth finger, and seals with his
    gore.
—You may guess that their chieftain shows stern
    discontent
When he gets nine petitions, each asking consent
For the writer, his vassal, his service to quit
On some pretext "so urgent it cannot admit
Of delay;"—though chagrined, he perforce must
    agree;
"Shikanosuké's to blame for *this* move," mutters he,
"If they wish it, however, I'll let them go free;"—

So he yields—that same ev'ning, when night's growing
    late,
Ten retainers file out through the ponderous gate,
And at daybreak ten *rônin*,⁶ concealed on the hill
In the rear of the castle, lurk watchful and still!

    And how does Kokonoyé take
        Her lover's evil plight?
    Poor girl! her heart is like to break,
        She sobs from morn till night;
    With hair dishevelled—swollen eyes—
        And cheeks with tear-drops wet—
    In truth, you'd hardly recognize
        Our former bright coquette!
While her lover's a *rônin*, her father, beguiled
By the wily *karô*, has now suddenly smiled
On the suit that that hypocrite dares to prefer
To *herself*, Shikanosuké's betrothed—yes, to *her*!
'Out of sight, out of mind,' says the proverb, you know;
Now his rival is absent, he thinks he's a 'show'
To go courting himself, for her favor to plead,—
With her sire on his side, he's convinced he'll succeed;—
But there's yet one more proverb that's equally clear,
Which remarks—'Lost to sight, yet to memory dear;'
And the Councillor finds, to his rage and his shame,
That he *can't* shake her trust in her victimized 'flame'!
    Then, his temper to try,
    And his threats to defy,
Kokonoyé's backed up by a trusty ally—

---

6. *Rônin*,—the name given to a man who, for some offence, had been dismissed from the service of his feudal lord,—or who, in some cases, had voluntarily gone into exile.

'Tis her grandma, the nun, who thus 'comes to the fore,'
For she hates Terutsura like poison—and more!
On the night Shikanosuké went forth in disgrace,
This benevolent dame in his pocket did place
A full purse,—and besides, as a sorrowful treat,
She contrived that the lovers a last time should meet!
Shikanosuké was agonized, crazy with grief—
Kokonoyé in torrents of tears found relief—
Scarce a word could they utter, yet amply expressed
Were the feelings that filled each disconsolate breast!
That last interview's memories fully avail
To ensure a deaf ear to the Councillor's tale;
Kokonoyé's relentless, with scorn in her eyes
She repels his advances, and angrily cries,

    "She'd rather roam the mountains cold
      "By Shikanosuké's side,
    "Than share a throne of gems and gold
      "As Terutsura's bride!"

Madam Seigan, the nun, as I've mentioned before,
Takes her grand-daughter's part, and then quickly wins o'er
Lady Yayé, our heroine's mother, to sign
A defensive alliance;—the ladies combine,—
    All their influence use
    The *karô* to abuse,—
And ere long their tormentor quite shakes in his shoes;
For if Tomita's lord should e'er chance to suspect
His retainer's vile schemes, or his motives detect,
Then 'adieu' to ambition, wealth, rank he must say,—
'Twill, in fact, be a case of the *oni*[7] to pay!

---

7. *Oni*,—devil, or demon.

LADY KOKONOYÉ.

    So he sits himself down
    With a curse and a frown,
Puts his conjuring cap on, and cudgels his brains
To devise some fresh plan—and not long he remains;
For there's *some one* we know is uncommonly quick
To assist those whose conscience at nothing will stick!
    Up he springs in delight—
    "That's the ticket! all right!
" I'll arrange the whole matter this very same night;—
"Ay! when *he's* safe removed, I'll soon manage the
    crew
"Of old hags,—and then, ho! my proud beauty, for
    you!"
So he writes a long letter, and seals it with care,
Calls a page, gives him secret commands to beware
That no soul shall the errand or sender divine,
Packs him off, and then seats himself calmly to dine;
—And the strangest of all strange events, I'll allow,
Is the fact that this rascal's not choked by his 'chow'!

    Throughout the spacious castle hall
        Reign fear and consternation;
    The vassals whisper, beck, and call
        In gloomy perturbation;
    And Yoshihisa ill conceals
        His manifest vexation,
    While Terutsura's face reveals
        A smile of exultation!
"Room! Room! for the Envoy!"—the vassals divide
In two ranks—down the hall comes, with leisurely
    stride,

Ura Hiôbu-no-jô, stately, tall and refined,
With his silk *naga-bakama*[8] trailing behind,—
Squats in front of the dais with dignity proud,
Draws a scroll from his bosom, and reads it aloud:—
    "You, Yoshihisa, of the line
      "Of Amako"—('tis writ)
    "Of Tomita, in Idzumo,
      "The present lord, to wit!—
    "WHEREAS, Our ears have lately heard
      "Strange tales of grievance spoke,
    "And high and low have plaints preferred
      "Against your cruel yoke,—
    "NOW THEREFORE, it is Our command
      "You presently be set
    "Within a cage, bound foot and hand,
      "And covered with a net,
    "And to Our Capital be sent,
      "Where We shall then decide
    "For you a fitting punishment,
      "All as the laws provide!"—
With a groan Yoshihisa falls forward, as flat
As a pancake, and presses his face to the mat;
While his vassals dismayed, with alarm in their eyes,
Clearly show that the news takes them quite by
    surprise.
What!—their lord, so benevolent, kindly, and just,
To be trussed like a fowl, and in prison be thrust!
It's preposterous!—some one has slandered him!—here
The cry "Room for the Envoy!" again greets their
    ear,—

---

8. *Naga-bakama*.—long nether garments, trailing behind the feet for a yard or more, worn with the old court costume.

THE FALSE ENVOY.

Down they bow to the floor—they can't see, they don't
    think
That that Envoy's left eye gives a sinister wink
(Which some secret arrangement right plainly reveals)
As he passes the spot where the Councillor kneels!

    Oh! a dreary sight is seen next morn,
        When before the Castle gate
    The retainers sad, with looks forlorn,
        For their lord's departure wait!
Terutsura alone seems inclined to be gay,—
He has just seen the Envoy again on his way,
And he now hastens on, with remarkable zeal,
Yoshihisa's departure—not seeming to feel
        Any sorrow or grief,
        He just bundles his chief
(Who's half stupefied still with dismay and affright)
In the net-covered litter,[9] and shuts him in tight,—
Quickly starts him away, and then, pausing awhile
As the captive's borne off, gives a chuckle and smile,
And so turns on his heel with a satisfied smirk,
Like a man who's accomplished some arduous work;
"That was splendidly done," mutters he,—"and this
    hour
"Sees the proud Kokonoyé at last in my power!
Were you ever "up country," kind reader?—While
    there
You have probably noticed the *kago*—a chair
Made of slender bamboos, which is slung from a strong
Wooden pole, and so borne by two coolies along—

---

9. When a Japanese noble was to be conveyed to any place under guard, a net, usually of dark-green silk, was thrown over the *norimono* or litter in which he was borne.

'Tis a picturesque kind of conveyance—but say,
Did you ever yet *try* one, and ride a short way?
    If you did, I've no doubt
    That you quickly jumped out,
And with half-broken vertebræ, quite benumbed shin,
Roundly cursed your own folly that e'er you got in!
And you felt, I'll be bound, in your tortured condition,
'Twas an engine quite worthy the old Inquisition!
    Torquemada, I'll swear,
    Had it chanced that he e'er
Clapped his eyes on this most diabolical chair,
Would his pincers, racks, pulleys, and all have displaced,
And to each of his victims have given a taste
    Of the *kago*, instead!
    To begin with, your head
Is so bumped 'gainst the pole that you're stunned and half-dead;
Then your neck is all twisted awry, and your feet
Go to sleep, and your chin and your knees almost meet;
And you writhe and you turn, in your efforts to ease
Your poor bones, and so doing, your coolies displease,—
Till they audibly growl, and then angrily swear
At the 'squirms' and the twists of their troublesome 'fare'!
But conceive, now, what agony yet you'd endure
If your limbs were bound tightly!—that done, I am sure
Yoshihisa's condition will wring from your breast
A deep sigh—he's not happy, that must be confessed.

About a *ri*[10]
They've gone, when he
  Is suddenly aware
Of an angry shout,
And a noise and rout
  Beside his prison chair;
'Tis a beggar bold,
Who has plainly strolled
  For miles the road along,
Now makes essay
To force his way
  Right in amongst the throng,
And before the stern guards can arrest him, he's seen
At the side of the litter, and in through the screen
Quickly pops a short dirk!—then commences a fray,—
"Cut him down!"—"Knock him over!"—they angrily
    say,
As they rush on him fiercely—what's this! from
    beneath
His straw coat a long sword flashes out from its
    sheath;
How he slashes and thrusts!—but a moment, no more,
And the guards take to flight, and the combat is o'er,—
Sauve qui peut—off they scamper—behind, in full chase,
Runs the beggar, intent upon 'forcing the pace'!

Yoshihisa, of course, now a weapon he's got,
Cuts asunder his bonds, and is out like a shot;
  While he stands, in surprise
  At his freedom, his eyes
Note a strange-looking form from a thicket arise:—

---

[10]. A Japanese measure of length, equal to about 2½ English miles.

Is't a robber?—yet, surely that visage we know,—
'Tis the former Court Envoy, the Hiôbu-no-jô!
Down he drops on his knees at the *daimiô's* feet,
And with tears in his eyes does for pardon entreat:
What! for pardon?—yes, quickly the scheme he does
    tell—
How the *soi-disant* Envoy was nought but a 'sell.'—
How the wicked *karô* had induced him to play
The false *rôle*, with intent the poor lord to betray—
How, the hoax at an end, to his horror and grief
He has learned Yoshihisa's his brother's old chief,
(For his brother, it seems, of the *rônin* is one)—
How he longs to amend all the mischief he's done;
And, to prove his contrition, his crimes to repair,
He now offers to guide my lord Amako where
He may meet with safe shelter and suitable fare;—
Yoshihisa accepts, with delight in his heart,
So the robber and noble together depart.

But while all this is passing, our heroine bold
Has resolved to escape from the Councillor's hold;
Her dislike's changed to horror, for rightly she deems
She herself is the object of all his vile schemes.
Oh! for brave Shikanosuké to guard her from ills!
Shikanosuké? alas! he's now roaming the hills—
    Ha! a thought strikes her brain—
    Could *she* manage to gain
That same hill, she may hope safely hid to remain
Till he once more shall meet her—he's not far
    away:—
(How she knows *that*, fair reader, 'tis not mine to
    say;

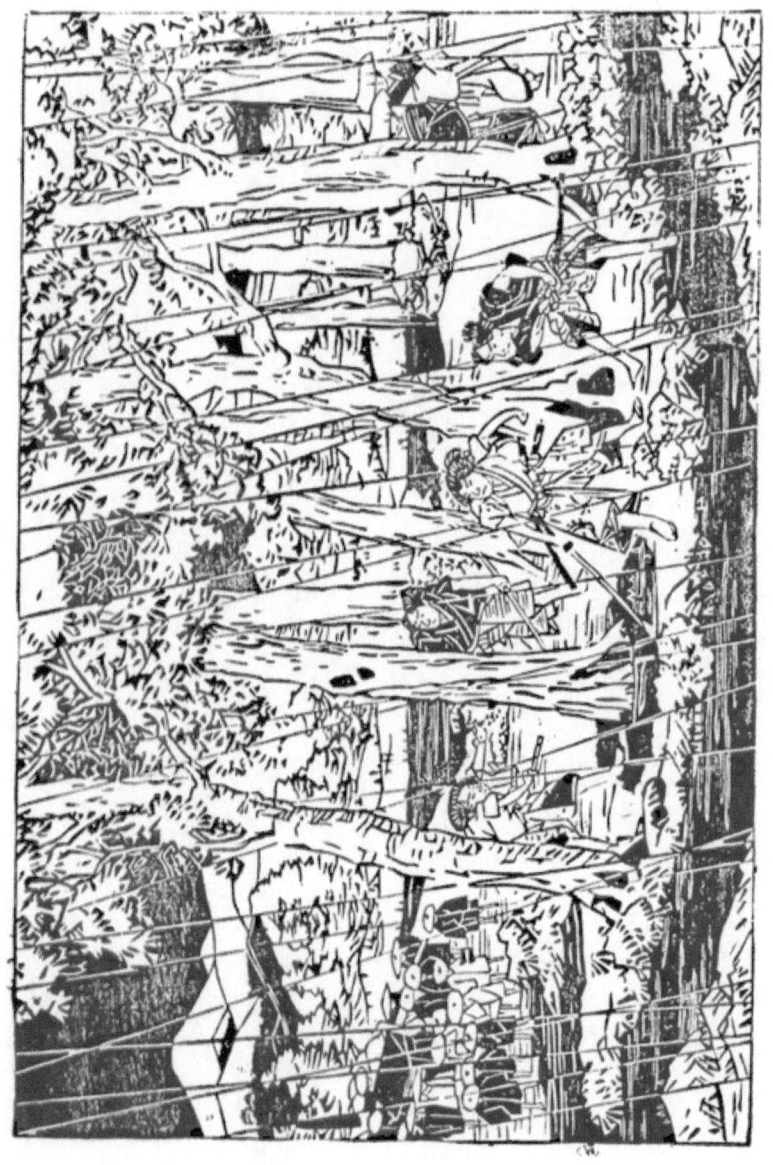

IN AMBUSH.

But this much I may hint, that some fond *billet-doux*
May *perhaps* have assured her her lover is true!)
    Quickly thought, quickly done—
     To her mother she's run,
Has confided her hopes,—and the morrow's bright sun
Sees her far from the castle, her journey begun :—
Let us hope she'll succeed in her desperate plan,
Now, Diogenes-like, she's 'in search of a man!'

    On a lone, dark plain,
    'Mid the sleet and rain,
      Beneath yon sombre tree,
    See! sword in hand
    The *rónin* stand
      By *one*—by *two*—by *three;*
By *four*—by *five*,
They still arrive,
    And silently they wait,
Till soon they spy
Yet more draw nigh,
    By *six*—by *seven*—by *eight;*
Their number's told—
We plain behold
    Our half-score 'valiant men,'—
Ay, there they stand,
That outlawed band,
    By *nine*—and eke by *ten!*
'Tis a terrible sight, for we clearly can see
That there's murder, for certain, upon the *tapis!*
—Hark, a step!—quick they dodge 'neath the dark
    leafy screen,

Whence they get a good view, yet themselves are unseen :
And two wayfarers, weary, and cold, and wet through,
All be-splashed and be-mired, slowly come into view ;
Why, who's this ?—mark that face !—no, it never can be—
Yet it *is*—Kokonoyé !—alas, it is she !
Poor, forlorn little damsel !—is *this*, then, the end
Unto which all her fond dreams of happiness tend ?—
Overcome by fatigue, with a gasp and a groan
Down she sinks in the mire, and lies still as a stone ;
While her nurse (her companion) in grief and despair
Falls to wringing her hands, and to tearing her hair !
—Is there none to give aid ?—through the fast-pouring rain
She perceives in the distance a gentleman's train ;
Loud she calls for assistance—they quickly arrive,
At the moment our heroine seems to revive ;
    But alas ! a worse woe
    Now awaits her—for lo !
In the litter there sits the inhuman *karô !*—
'Tis the *Councillor*'s voice that in loud mocking strain
Cries, "Aha ! my fair truant !—I've caught you again !"
—And our heroine finds, to her grief and her ire,
She's but 'out of the frying pan into the fire' !

    The nurse in abject fear does whine ;
      Her charge erect remains—
    The proud old blood of all her line
      Now boils within her veins—

Her eyes fixed sternly on her foe's,
  (Who half-abashed does pause)
With hand that now no falt'ring knows
  Her dagger keen she draws—
And she'll *use* it, be sure, in a way he can feel,
For the Amako race were aye prone to draw steel!
Undecided he halts—when a crash and a rout
Greet his ear, and a voice cries with menacing shout,
  "Thou traitor, stand!—thy flight is flown!
  "Release my lady dear!—
  "Now, Terutsura, hold thine own,
  "For Shikanosuké's here!"—
  Vain, vain his skill!—his weapon's aid
    Can scarce avert his fate,
  Ere the swing of our hero's practised blade
    Descends upon his pate!
Down he goes, dead as mutton! while loudly around
Do the clashing and din of hot combat resound;
For the *rônin* rush in like wild tigers, and then
They make mincemeat, in short, of the Councillor's men!
Shikanosuké alone takes no part in the fight—
He has something far better to do,—and he's right;
  Quick his left arm is placed
  Round the slim willow-waist
Of his lady-love—backward he draws her in haste;
They regard with indifference foeman and friend,
And they don't seem to care how the battle may end—
What they say to each other, you e'en may suppose
For yourselves—*I* can't tell you, for nobody knows:

Yet they *seem* to be anything rather than 'blue'—
But the curtain here falls, and they're hid from our
    view!

L'Envoye to the Reader.

"I do not rhyme to that dull elf"
(Sir Walter here I quote)
"Who cannot image to himself"
What I have failed to note ;—
How, of course, Shikanosuké it was who had freed
Yoshihisa, in moment of danger and need ;
How the latter, in gratitude, kindly did smile
On our fond pair, and blessed them in 'stage father's'
    style ;
How they all went their way ;
How, from that happy day,
Kokonoyé was never again known to stray
From her home, but looked after her *fils* and *mari*
In a mode that was really quite touching to see ;
And how, *jure uxoris*, that gallant young man
In due space became chief of the Tomita clan ;
And how, e'en to this time, are their praises yet
    told ;—
Kokonoyé the fair—Shikanosuké the bold !

THE
HAUNTED MANSION.

THE main facts of this terrible tragedy are, alas! but too true. It occurred during the spring of the year 1653, in the town mansion of one Awoyama Shuzen, an official of the then-existing Police Bureau. This mansion is still standing in Tôkiô, and the fatal well also exists even at the present time; the ghost, however, has fortunately ceased to haunt the premises.

#

From the Original Japanese Play of "Banchô Sara-yashiki," as Performed at the Shimabara Theatre, Tôkiô, in August, 1878.

    SILENT it stands.   No sound of voice
        Is heard within the door;
    No tramp of steed, or armèd men,
        As in the days of yore;
    The night-owl flaps his heavy wing
        Beneath the sombre trees,
    Unbarred the massive portals swing
        Before the ev'ning breeze.

    No gallant throng of vassals bold
        Is there, the eye to greet;
    Closed are the windows once that looked
        Upon the busy street;
    No warder now his vigil keeps,
        No watchman goes his round,
    Still as the tomb the mansion sleeps,
        Of life no sign, no sound!

Would'st hear of those who erst did in it dwell?—
Then list, kind Reader, while the tale I tell.

Years ago, in Japan, then, here let it be told,
There resided a nobleman, wealthy and bold ;
Otogawa his surname ; his Christian name—well,
I'm ashamed to confess that I simply can't tell ;
But I hope the omission you'll pardon this time,
For these names do not always fit in with one's
    rhyme.
        —I may mention, too, here
        It's perhaps rather queer
To be talking of *Christian* names, seeing 'tis clear
That the style of religion then commonly known
Was decidedly Buddhist or Shintô in tone ;
(Though the Buddhists, to-day, are as poor as can
    be—
'Disestablished,' you know, during '73)—
Well, it chanced that this noble received one fine
    day
From the Shôgun some curio (*what*, I can't say),
And was ordered to hold it in keeping discreet,
Till his lord should reclaim it, and give a receipt.
Now, Japan is a land, I am forced to reveal,
Where the robber right often doth 'break through and
    steal' ;
        To our noble's dismay,
        He discovered one day
That his charge had ta'en wings, and had flown right
    away,—
Nought remained save the casket that once it did fill,
'Twas a clear case of *box, et præterea nil !*
        He fell into disgrace,
        First at Court lost his place,
Then was turned out of doors with a very long face,

And was fain, in the end, for safe shelter to fly
To the house of one Sampei, a young *samurai*;
Here he lay in concealment, to cover his shame,
And was joined by his wife—Hanazono her name,—
While his vassals of course quickly melted away,
As the snow disappears 'neath the sun's scorching ray.
There was one of his clients was mightily glad
At the thought that his chieftain had 'gone to the bad;'
For this rogue, Asayama, had long been in league
With confederates cunning and apt at intrigue,
With intent to secure what he swore was his due,
Viz.—his lord's high position, and revenue too;
Now, his rival remov'd, he thought soon to rise straight
From a mere *hatamoto* to *daimiô*'s state.
At the time my tale opens, this villain decided
(Whom 'for short' we'll term Tessan) in Yedo resided,
In the district called Banchô,—which, ev'ry one knows,
Is chock-full of small *yashiki*[1] in rows upon rows,—
And there dwelt in his household a young serving-maid
Called O Kiku, a beauty, yet modest and staid;
She was bride to that Sampei I've mentioned above,
But by poverty forced from the side of her love.
—All this 'yarn,' gentle Reader, 's no part of the play,
But I've thought it as well just to put you *au fait*

---

1. *Yashiki*,—the fortified town-mansions of the Japanese feudal nobles.

THE HAUNTED MANSION.

With these facts, as the folks who've been introduced here
In the subsequent drama may chance to appear;
Still, it's time the performance were really begun—
Hark! the clapper sounds—" Hats off!"—'tis said and 'tis done,
And the curtain now rises on Scene No. 1.

    A charming garden greets our eye;—
      Green bushes, blossoms gay—
    Along a trellis, rear'd on high,
      The slender creepers stray—
    A rustic well—a garden stool—
      Old stones, with lichens gray—
    A tiny arbour, light and cool,
      And screen'd from noontide ray—
    " The very spot," in glee you cry,
      " To spend a summer's day!"
'Tis a ' Garden of Eden,' you'd almost believe;
But appearances oft times are apt to deceive,—
And I'm certain you'd speedily alter your mind
Could you view the dark form in yon arbour reclined!

    Dimly, through the lattice screen,
    Robes of rich brocade are seen;
    Faintly, too, the straining eye
    Can a human shape descry;
    There, in worst of angry moods,
    Haughty Tessan sits and broods—
    Broods o'er what?—o'er fancied wrong;
    Vowing vengeance, too, ere long!

You'll remember O Kiku, this mansion who graced?—
She was lovely as Venus, as Dian as chaste;
But it seems, not to put too fine point on the matter,
That her lord for some time past had cast sheep's eyes
    at her,
And it chanced, this same day, to her dire con-
    sternation,
Of his love he had made a downright declaration!
    Now old Horace, we know,
    Sang in years long ago
(When at school I'd have quoted the lines *comme il
    faut*,
But th' identical verse from my mem'ry now fades)
Of the loves of great heroes for fair serving-maids;
And, in fact, wrote a sonnet expressly to prove
How one '*serva Briseis*' so managed to 'move
By her snow-white complexion' her lord, as to catch
Young Achilles himself—no indifferent match :—
Whether Tessan read Latin or not's all the same,
But it's clear he'd attempted to play a like game,
And had 'taken a leaf from the book,' so to speak,
Of his classical model, the 'swift-footed' Greek!
With the *men*, though, all slight similarity ended;
For Briseis was willing,—O Kiku, offended!
(There, it's done!—I'm rejoiced to have 'scaped with
    whole skin,
Having ventured on ice so unpleasantly thin!)

    " When Poverty's gaunt form "—so runs
      The proverb—" to our eyes
    " Appears upon the threshold, Love
      " From out the window flies;"—

But conceive, if you *can*, a more terrible state
Of affairs than when Love is succeeded by Hate!
After deep cogitation, proud Tessan has laid
His vile schemes to chastise the poor innocent maid;
Long ago, it would seem, so the story relates,
He had placed in her charge just a decade of plates
(He was great upon porcelain, this reprobate man)
Of the best willow-pattern that's known in Japan;
    —(You right often, I ween
    Gentle reader, have seen
Such a style,—the two islands—the waters between,
Straddled o'er by a bridge—in the distance a boat—
And the peach-tree and doves you've not failed, too, to
    note)—
Of the ten, he's contrived *one* to slily regain,
And has then, in a manner quite barefaced and plain,
Falsely taxed the poor girl, of her wits half-bereft,
With committing a downright and palpable theft;
And he now sits in state, to determine the crime,
To accuse and condemn at the very same time!
    And just beneath—accomplice meet!—
      The vassal Chiuda stands;
    With loins girt up, and sandalled feet,
      To bear his lord's commands:
    Macaulay's words come *à propos*
      Of two such evil men—
    Take down his 'Lays of Ancient Rome,'
      Con o'er the leaves, and then
    In that sad tale 'Virginia'
      'Tis writ, you'll plainly see,
    That "wheresoe'er such lord is found,
      "Such client still will be!"

"Bring forth the culprit!"—from afar
　A gruff response one hears;
　In single file, a dismal train
　　Upon the stage appears:—
Goodness me! is that Kiku?—What awful hard lines
To be bound with that cord that her shoulders entwines!
And,—oh, horror!—her six vile attendants!—just see
How they gloat o'er their prey with unprincipled glee!
'Pon my word, it would cause any Christian to swear,
Just to note the stout cudgels the ruffians bear!
　　　Not regarding her woe,
　　　On the ground just below
The small arbour, poor Kiku they cruelly throw;
And then Chiuda commences, in manner irate,
To enquire "what the dickens she's done with that plate?"
She don't know that it's lost;—she declares it's all right—
That the number's complete—that she's innocent quite—
Whereupon Mr. Chiuda, without more ado,
Tips the wink to the rest of the villanous crew,
When each *brute* (for I certainly cannot say *man*)
Falls upon her and 'lams' her as hard as he can,
Showing no more compunction, nor heed to her pain,
Than as if he were thrashing a bushel of grain!
Thus admonished, she's bidden anew to confess,—
Not a bit of it,—spite of her grief and distress,
She protests she's no thief,—"if her lord be so kind
"As to count o'er the plates, the full number he'll find."

Quickly Tessan hands over a box at his side,
(Made of rich gilded lacquer, with silken cord tied)—
"There, then; count for yourself!—Take them out one by one,
"Chiuda, slowly—'tis time that this nonsense were done!"
(Here in rapt expectation the audience waits,
While O Kiku begins telling over the plates.)

'*One!*' from Chiuda;—from Kiku, '*One!*'—'*One!*' Tessan cries;
Down it goes on the ground 'fore the whole trio's eyes:
Number *two* next succeeds,—and then *three*,—and then *four*,—
And so on till they've reckoned just five of them more,—
"That is *nine!* where's the *tenth* one?" with agonized cry
The poor creature exclaims;—Chiuda raises on high
Th' empty casket, reversed, and shouts fiercely, "*Mo nai!*"[2]
And there passes o'er Tessan's dark visage a smile,
As he hails the success of his infamous wile!
    —Oh! the scene that ensues!
    How the wretches abuse
Their unfortunate victim!—completely they lose
All humanity, pity, and mercy as well,
And are changed into demons,—aye, demons of hell!
—I will spare you the details;—suffice it to say
She is slung in mid air, in a barbarous way,

---
[2]. "No more!"

O'er the well, and the vassals, retiring, await
While their lord with his prey has a short *tête-à-tête*;
'Tis a last chance he gives her—yet nought does he
    gain;
She is true to her spouse, spite of torture and pain;—
"Well then, die!" yells the monster, "by Sandzu's [3]
    dark tide
"Master Sampei's arrival not long shall you bide!"—
    A flash!—a shriek prolonged and shrill!—
        Is *no one* nigh to aid?—
    Half-crazed with rage, he madly waves
        Aloft his trenchant blade—
    A thud—an agonizing groan
        (Thank Heav'n! 'tis only *one*)—
    A rushing fall—a heavy plunge—
        The dreadful deed is done!

Mr. Chiuda commences with speed to efface
Of the horrible murder all record and trace;
First he cleanses the sword-blade with dexterous hand,
Next he rinses the stones, and then splashes the sand,
Till there's no tell-tale stain on the ground to be seen,
And the whole of the garden looks tidy and clean:
Stay! a spot yet remains—how o'erlook'd I can't
    tell—
So his bucket once more clatters into the well.

        (Hush! what was that?—from 'neath the ground
            Proceeds a stifled moan—
        Then, louder still, a dismal sound,
            A weird, sepulchral tone!

---

3. The River Sandzu,—the Buddhist Styx.

THE HAUNTED WELL.

Hark! a horrible voice on our tympanum grates—
'Tis the voice of a woman a-counting of plates!)

    Haul, Chiuda, haul!—the bucket's raised;—
      A yell of wild despair!—
    What ails him?—is the fellow crazed?—
      Slight wonder if he were!—
    See, see!—yon fearsome, awful sight!
      A form, with bosom bare—
    With hands and face of ghastly white—
      With dank, dishevelled hair—
    With wide, deep gash to view displayed
      Across her throat so fair—
    Oh, horror! 'tis O Kiku's shade
      That grins and gibbers there!
With a shriek of affright, and a wild frantic bound,
Mr. Chiuda, half-swooning, falls flat on the ground!
        When the ghost, for awhile,
        Looks around with a smile
Of revenge,—then, in true pyrotechnical style,
Disappears down the well (which yawns open to greet
    her)
With a fizz, and a bang, and a smell of salt-petre!

    "I beseech you, my lord, not a moment to waste!
    " Pray retire to your other large mansion in haste!
    "*This* is haunted!—ah me!—oh, the ghost!—do
        not wait!"
    —Here a crowd of retainers file in through the
        gate:—
    " Well, I'm off," cries his chieftain, " without more
        delay;"

"And I'll go too," says Chiuda;—" Excuse me,
    you'll *stay!*
" Keep your pecker up, man, and you can't come
    to harm,
" For you'll find a stout stomach will act as a
    charm."
    Off he goes with his men ;
    Chiuda rises, and then
Gives a startled glance upwards—what is it he sees
That so soon brings him down again plump on his
    knees?
Look! he's speechless with terror—as white as a
    post—
What's that *form* floating o'er him ?—" Help! *Murder!*
    the GHOST !"
—We can guess pretty well how the circumstance
    ends,
For a loud scream is heard as the curtain descends.

Mr. Chiuda has seemingly managed to 'fix'
His assailant, and now is again at his tricks,
    For in Scene No. 2
    He's revealed to our view,
Safe and sound—and in precious bad company, too ;
For there stands at his side, in a narrow by-street,
Such a blackguardly 'rough' as you'd rather not
    meet
Of a dark wintry night, on a moorland remote,—
That's to say, if you've any regard for your throat !
At a glance it's apparent, and well understood
That the brace of sly rascals are up to no good ;

THE CONSPIRATORS.

From the words that we catch,
'Twould appear that they're hatch-
ing a plot that for cold-blooded slaughter might match
With the massacre which, so historians say,
Was enacted in France one Bartholomew's day!
First, a purse changes hands—
Then come Chiuda's commands,
Fully detailed on paper, that nought go amiss—
And the gist of the scheme, gentle Reader, is this ;—
Mr. Takurô (so's named the rough whom we see,
And the uncle, moreover, of Sampei is he)
Is to wait an occasion, as best to his mind,
And then murder his nephew and all he may find
'Neath his roof-tree,—in fact, he's to 'go for' the pack of 'em,
And to 'wipe out' the household, aye, ev'ry man jack of 'em!
Oh! there never was heard such a bloodthirsty thing!
And I'd venture to swear
That, though Tessan's not there,
He is still the prime mover who's pulling the string!

Scene the Third.—Sampei's parlour to view is display'd,
Where his sister O Miné (a dear little maid)
With the wife of our friend Otogawa is talk-
ing at home, while the men folks are out for a walk.
Hark! a bang at the gate!
Hanazono is straight
Bundled into a cupboard, there hidden to wait

Till the visitor's gone,—then the door's opened wide;
Enter Takurô, marching with swaggering stride.
—He's a sly fellow, Takurô;—what do you think?
He's perceived the whole scene through an opportune chink!—
How he blusters, fumes, threatens, and swears in a breath!
Poor O Miné's on tenter-hooks, frightened to death:—
"Ha! ha! *what's in the cupboard?* here, quick! let me see,—
"Stand aside, Miss, I tell you!—d'you think to 'bluff' me?—
　　　"Ho! ho! just as I thought,—
　　　"Now the pretty bird's caught,—
"Come! get out of your nest there, unless you'd be brought!"
　　　Never heeding her squalls
　　　Or her screams, as she bawls
For "Police!" Hanazono he speedily hauls
From her hiding-place—now there commences a scene!
Look! her ladyship scutters beneath a tall screen,—
Then behind the *hibachi* [4] a refuge does take!
What a noise and a hubbub the three of them make!
How they dodge their pursuer! how angrily he
Gives them chase, in a mode quite exciting to see!
　　　As he's close on their track
　　　There resounds a loud 'whack,'
And the villain goes down with a thump on his back!
While a nicely dressed gentleman, bowing before them,

---

4. *Hibachi*,—brazier, or fire-box.

Bids the ladies take courage, as he will watch o'er
    them :—
" Beg your pardon, My Lady :— your lord is my
    friend ;
" He has charged me in haste at this house to attend,
" And to offer my escort to point out the way
" To a fresh place of refuge he's chosen to-day ;
      " You'll no doubt feel surprise
      " At my words, but your eyes
" Will the token he's sent you at once recognise ;
" 'Tis this charm-case,—I'm ordered to show it to you,
" As a proof, if required, that my errand is true ;
" In the litter with which my retainers here wait
" You can ride in a manner beseeming your state.
" By your leave, then—allow me—please follow, I
    pray—
" And you, villain, d'ye hear me ?—get out of the way !
" Ha ! you *will* have it then ! "—and his sword in a
    trice
Has half leapt from its scabbard—too close to be nice,
As our friend Mr. Takurô cannot but feel,
(For the bully, 'twould seem, has a dread of cold
    steel)
So he bounds to one side with uncommon dexterity, .
And then bolts for the kitchen with wondrous celerity ;
      While his foe, with a face
      Full of smiles, and a grace-
ful obeisance, escorts his fair charge to her place
In the gay gilded norimon—pulls down the blind—
Bids his vassals close up, both in front and behind—
Gives the word—and she's borne off as swift as the
    wind !

And O Miné—in Takurô's mercies so tender ?—
Not at all; here's her father come home to befriend her.
  He at first is opprest
  With alarm for his guest,
But his daughter explains, and his mind's set at rest;
  They sit down to their tea;
  (My fair readers may see
What a time-honored treat must the 'kettledrum' be!)
Sajidaiyu (the father)'s just put out of sight
His first cup, with a gulp, and a hiss of delight
A la mode japonaise (the true sound I can't give,
But I fancy it's known to most persons who live
  In the isles of Japan)
  When a queer little man
Clad in gray, with a staff, and a huge pedlar's pack
That is strapped by stout cords on his feeble old back,
Puts his head through the door with a smirk and a grin,
And proceeds to enquire 'if there's anyone in.'
"What! old Rokubu!—welcome! what fortune to meet you!
"Pray be seated—we're always delighted to greet you;
"You're a regular stranger—you're up and you're down,
"And you're ev'rywhere, save in our part of the town!
"Why, it seems quite an age since your face I last saw!
—"And what news do you bring from my daughter-in-law?"

EVIL TIDINGS.

Sighs with grief the agèd one,
  Vainly strives to speak—
Briny tears in torrents run
  Down his furrowed cheek—
Scarce a word can he reply
  To their greeting kind—
Only broken sobs imply
  Dire distress of mind :
From the bundle at his side,
  With a look of pain,
Forth he draws a garment, dyed
  Deep with crimson stain ;—
"*This* is all my tidings sore,
  "*This* the news I bear—
"'Tis your murder'd daughter's gore
  "Dyes her mantle there !"—
Here, I'll frankly confess, my Muse utterly fails
To describe with decorum the shrieks and the wails,
  And the howls and the groans,
  And the sobs and the moans,
And the curses, too, mutter'd in scarce smother'd
  tones,
That are wrung from both father and daughter as well
As they list to the tale that their guest has to tell !
So suffice it to mention that, could he behold
All the anguish he's wrought, even Tessan the bold
Some degree of remorse would most certainly feel
At the sight—and you'll own that that means a good
  deal !
  Sajidaiyu first dries
    His wet cheeks and his eyes,
Wipes his nose on his sleeve, and then hastily flies

Through the gate, down the roadway, in quest of his
    son,
To acquaint him at once with the deed that's been
    done;
    While O Miné, midst all
      That has chanced to befall,
Still remembers (though late) hospitality's call,
And at last with a gulp having managed to sub-
due her grief, asks her guest 'if he'd like a hot tub;'—
He assents;—as they both through the door disappear,
Mr. Takurô, seeing the coast is all clear,
Re-emerges—what's up?—why, I'm bound to confess
That his aim is to 'prig' poor O Kiku's silk dress!
" Here's the bundle I noted that old buffer drop—
" If it only contain something handy to 'pop'!
" What! a nasty wet dress!—and with stains on it
    too—
" Why, it's cover'd with *blood!*—what a regular 'do'!
" *Chez mon oncle*, I'll swear, 'twouldn't fetch half a
    *bu!*⁵
" Ugh! it's giv'n me the creeps!"—so his prize he lets
    fall,
Then with patent disgust rolls it up in a ball,
And so hangs it, intact, from a peg on the wall.

By some lucky coincidence, here we discern
Otogawa and Sampei together return;
And the former—(there's mischief a-brewing, we see)—
Loudly calls for his *wife!*—not a word answers she—
('Twould be strange if she did, for she's now a
    good *ri*

---

5. 1 *bu*, about 25 cents.

On her journey)—"Hi! Minô! what means this
    strange trick?
"Where's her Ladyship?"—"Who?"—"Why, my
    wife—tell me quick!"—
"Then 'twas *not* your retainer who took her away?"—
"My retainer?—no! nonsense!—why, what's that you
    say
"'Bout a charm-case?—'tis mine!—one I lost t'other
    day!
"Oh, the villain!—he's used it no doubt to betray
"The poor girl to my foes!—here's the devil to pay!
"Oh, the rogue!—quick, my sword!—oh, the mon-
    ster!—my dirk!
"I'll get even, though, with him for this bit of
    work!"—
    See! he bounds from the floor—
    Rushes out at the door—
Like a wild bull of Bashan, with shout and with roar
Of defiance!—O Miné close after him follows,
To his bass adds her treble, and plaintively 'holloas'!
(If she last at his pace, though, a marvel 't will be—
'Tis a case of *haud passibus æquis*, you see!)

Here's the chance for which Takurô's waited so long!
Hark! he 'goes for' his nephew in language that's
    strong,
Calls him 'blackguardly rascal' and 'reprobate
    vicious,'
And rebukes him for 'harbouring persons suspicious';
    He may bawl till he's hoarse,
    Sampei scorns him, of course,
So our bully next thinks of appealing to force;

See! he clutches his throat, and endeavours to dash
Out his brains with a *geta !*[6] —when, sudden, a flash
From behind—and the villain goes down with a crash!
And the pedlar stands o'er him with gibe and with
    laugh,
And wipes down a long sword he's drawn out from
    his staff;
While he shows to young Sampei a letter he's found,
(It is Chiuda's) which Takurô dropped on the ground,
So it seems, as he lately the bundle unwound!
As the prospect of death his wild spirit depresses,
Mr. Takurô ' makes a clean breast,' and confesses
    All the plot, without fail;
    He's scarce finished his tale
When he turns on his stomach as dead as a nail!
Exit Rokubu, also to join in the chase—
There remains only Sampei, with woebegone face.

By the queer code of honor that guides *samurai*
Mr. Sampei now deems it his duty to die;
Here's his uncle been killed in his house!—plain as day
He's convinced that *his* life, too, the forfeit should pay;
Never mind about Rokubu—he's not detected,
'Tis improbable quite that he'll e'er be suspected:—
So our hero commences, without loss of time,
To prepare straight to ' cut himself off in his prime';
And, in fashion approved, he proceeds first to frame
A long document, taking the whole of the blame
On his own single shoulder;—this testament bold
He proposes to leave where his friends may behold
And peruse it, long after himself's dead and cold!

---

6. *Geta*,—a wooden clog.

Was that the wind?—no sound is heard—
 The night is silent all—
What was't that yonder garment stirred
 That's hanging from the wall?
See! from the bloodstained mantle float
 A ghastly phantom slow!—
O Kiku's self!—her face, we note,
 Bears trace of grief and woe;
With yearning gestures, longing eyes,
 She flits behind her mate—
Now waves, now beckons, vainly tries
 To lure him from his fate!
Fast speeds his pen across the sheet—
 He'll neither look nor hear—
While lies that charm-case at his feet,
 She dare not venture near!
Fast speeds the pen—he's ceased to write—
 Once more his head is reared—
The ghost has vanished from our sight,
 The phantom's disappeared!

All is ready—the critical moment draws nigh;—
First he bows to the altar—a pray'r and a sigh
Lets escape in a breath—lays the scroll on the floor,
Chucks the charm-case aside at the back of the door,
Sits him down with a smile to his terrible work,
Doffs his mantle and vest, and unsheathes his sharp
 dirk!
 —He lifts his hand—a sudden grasp
 Arrests the fatal blow!
 The dirk falls harmless from his clasp
 Upon the mat below!

>   Who's this?—he stares in wild surprise—
>   Howe'er did this betide?
>   A well-known figure greets his eyes—
>   O Kiku's at his side!
>   E'en as she lived, in habit gay,
>   Returns she to our view—
>   " My love! my dearest husband! say,
>   " What means this deed you'd do?"

Can you fancy the stare of an amorous fop,
Who has screwed up his courage and ventured to
    'pop,'
When he gets in reply not the word he's expected,
But a 'No' 'stead of 'Yes,' and is flatly rejected?
Or imagine the look on a keen jockey's face,
Who has thought himself certain of winning the
    race,
But discovers, alas! when the numbers are read,
He's been 'done in the eye' on the post by a head?
>   You may picture all these,
>   And e'en more, if you please,

But you *can't* fancy Sampei's queer 'phiz' when he
    sees
He's detected attempting to take a French leave,
And to cause his poor wife as a widow to grieve!
So he puts up his dirk, lays it back in its place,
And then hangs down his head like a boy in
    disgrace;—
When he raises his eyes—no O Kiku is there!
She has seized the occasion to melt into air!
>   See! he can't make it out—
>   How he rushes about!

Hear him call—and entreat—and then lustily shout!
Not a word in reply to his clamor and rout.
—Here his father comes back, and is startled to learn
The remarkable news of O Kiku's return;
        In a trice he narrates
        All the tale of the plates,
And of Tessan and Chiuda—" the vile reprobates,"
Till, in fact, he convinces his listener keen
That 'tis only the ghost of poor Kiku he's seen;
But as both are indulging in howls of despair,
See! O Miné flies in with a terrified air,
Hotly chased by a grim-looking murderous elf
With a sword in his grasp—why, 'tis Chiuda himself!
His accomplice not having fulfilled his command,
He has come with th' intention of lending a hand
To the foul work of slaughter so cunningly planned!—
Quickly Sampei springs forward to grapple his foe,
In a moment they've closed—see! they rock to and
    fro,
And then down on the mats in fierce struggle they go!
        How they tug and they strain!
        We can see pretty plain,
That whoe'er may the victory finally gain,
Won't at all be disposed to his foe to give grace—
Just observe the clench'd teeth, and each murderous
    face!
How they kick, punch, gouge, wrestle, belabour, and
    bite!
Oh! there never was seen such a rattling 'free fight'!
        But it's clear, all the same,
        That though Sampei be 'game,'
He's no match for his rival's superior frame—

He's outweighted—and oh! that last knock on his
    brow!
If there's no one to aid, 'tis U P with him now!
—Hark, a voice! at which Chiuda's wild frenzy
    abates—
'Tis the voice of a woman a-counting of plates!

    Some one's near, we plain can tell!
    Whence that smoke—that sulph'rous smell?
    From the garment on the wall
    Forth there floats a phantom tall—
    Stern and grim, a form of dread
    Hovers o'er the villain's head!
    Angry features—eyes of fire—
    Threat'ning glance of hatred dire—
    Needs not these to tell us clear
    What's O Kiku's errand here!

With the swoop of a hawk on a dickey-bird small,
Down she darts upon Chiuda—(just hark to his bawl
For assistance!)—"You're *wanted!* there, make no
    ado—
"Having 'done for' proud Tessan, I've now come for
    you!"

How he raves in his terror—how wildly does storm!
How he slashes and hews at the shadowy form!
How he yells as it seems his attack to deride,
Moving nearer and nearer with swift silent glide!
What a shriek rends the air as it seizes him tight,
And he feels its cold clutch on his throttle alight!
Fairly madden'd by terror, by fear almost crazed,
He yet makes one last effort—his weapon is raised—

Down it comes with a frantic and desperate blow—
But that shadowy form no resistance does show,
And the sharp steel is sheathed, fairly up to the hilt,
In the villain's own carcass—fit meed for his guilt!
There he lies, stiff and stark, right in front of our
    friends—
And away flits the ghost—and the curtain descends!

Now, of course, gentle reader, I hardly need tell
That our play, begun sadly, yet terminates well:
You no doubt can conceive for yourself by this time,
E'en without any aid from my cantering rhyme,
That our friend Otogawa from danger soon frees
His adored Hanazono, and sets her at ease—
That the make-believe friend who enticed her away
Is th' identical thief who (see prologue I pray),
Stole the curio left in the nobleman's hold—
That it chances, of course, that this ruffian bold
Is attacked by young Sampei, and killed in the
    fight—
That the treasure's returned to its owner of right—
That my lord the Shōgun, when the facts are made
    plain,
Reinstates Otogawa in favor again—
And that Sampei, when tired of a widower's life,
Soon replaces O Kiku, and takes a new wife!
—If you *can't* conceive this, then I've right to com-
    plain,
For I fear that my tale has been told but in vain!

MORAL.

I.

Many folks (so I've *heard*) are addicted at times
To an innocent pastime called 'ringing the chimes';
Now, though that's quite *en règle* for once in a way,
For their warning and guidance a maxim I'd lay;
It is this—don't prolong either frolic or spree,
When the church clock strikes solemnly *one*, *two*, and *three!*

II.

Just a word to 'old residents'—kindly enough;
And that is—should you chance to reside on the Bluff,
Keep your 'weather eye peeled' when it gets to be late,
See your watchman's on duty, and lock up your *plate!*

THE ENCHANTED PALACE.

THIS Play is an adaptation of a portion of a popular novel, or fairy-tale, by the celebrated modern Japanese author Kiokutei Bakin. It affords an excellent idea of the general style of light literature in this country. We regret that we are unable to provide our readers with more detailed information as to the fame and the deeds of the clerical hero than is herein contained.

#

*A Fragment from the Original Japanese Play of "Saiyuki"
("A Trip in the West"), as Performed at the Saruwaka-
machi Theatre, Asakusa, Tôkiô, in October, 1878.*

WHERE'S the knight of heart so bold
    Dares invade the wizard's hold?
Who alone of mortal men
Dares approach the syren's den?
Where's the spirit shall not quail,
Dares the "Black Cloud Mountain" scale?
Where the hero?—quick, declare!—
Echo only answers, "Where?"

"And where *was* this said mountain?"—I sternly
    object
To commit myself, Reader, in any respect;
For, in fact, its position to demonstrate right
Is a task for which I am incompetent quite;—
    Yet this much will I say—
    Take your Atlas down, pray;
Now, just hit the west border of "spicy Cathay;"
(Have you got it?)—then, next, will you carefully
    scan
All the district from thence down to fair Hindostan;—

Well, 'twas *somewhere* 'bout there—beyond that, as
    I live,
Not the least information I'm able to give;
But this much I will swear—not a word I'll retract—
That there *was* such a mountain 's a positive fact!

    ·Huge, sombre, silent and sublime
        The " Black Cloud Mountain " frowned,
    A landmark till the end of time
        For countless leagues around;
    With massive form upreared on high,
    With crags that seemed to pierce the sky,
        So tall, so sharp they rose,—
    Its tow'ring peak, with cloudy wreath,
    Looked down on other hills beneath
        Its diadem of snows,
    As some gigantic champion, born
    Of godlike race, might glance with scorn
        On Lilliputian foes!

Yes, it looked very fine from a distance, I'll own,
As a king may look noble and grand on his throne;
But suppose that the monarch should order his men
Quick to lead you away to the scaffold,—how then?
Would you *still* call him " gracious?"—Believe me, my
    friends,
' To the view it is distance enchantment that lends!'
(Thus I freely translate the old proverb you know,
Running " *omne ignotum pro magnifico.*")
And just so this same mountain, though grand to the
    eye,
Was a different thing when one ventured too nigh;
For each person who wasn't contented to view it,

But endeavoured to climb it, had reason to rue it!
Many dozens of 'globe-trotters,' eager and proud,
Thought to gain some slight *kudos* by 'doing' "Black
   Cloud;"
Many dozens, I say, started off on the track,
("They'd be up in a jiffey, and down in a crack!")
But alas! for their boasting—they *never came back!*
   Like the sick lion's den
   Of which Horace makes men-
tion (Epistles, Lib. I,—but the line's slipped my ken),
Some *perhaps* may have 'scaped, but no soul came
   across 'em,
—As a rule 'twas "*vestigia nulla retrorsum!*"
   (That's the line, by the way,
   So historians say,
Was inscribed on John Hampden's war-banner so gay,
As a kind of a hint that he never would yield,
When he rode to his death on the famed Chalgrove
   Field.
—What a strange thing a man of John Hampden's
   fine stamp
Should have sided with Cromwell, that regicide
   scamp!)
   Oh! many a band,
   With "Murray" in hand,
Tried to scale those steep heights and that pinnacle
   grand—
Oh! many a party, and many a crowd,
Started off on a pic-nic to famous "Black Cloud"—
But they stayed there *for ever*, not merely *pro tem.;*
'Stead of 'doing' the mountain, the mountain 'did'
   them!

THE ENCHANTED PALACE.

Now it chanced, at that time, that in fair Hindostan
There resided a truly remarkable man ;
This was Sanzô, a priest, for his wisdom renowned,
For his virtue, his tact, and his learning profound :
He'd devoted his lifetime to clerical work,
And in fact was a pretty " big wig " in the kirk,
But I can't hit his title off right to the letter,
So I'll dub him the " Bishop " for want of a better.
    A gentle, kindly man was he,
        Who strove to labour right ;
    Indeed, he'd compass land and sea
        To make a proselyte :
    His high silk cap was fashioned well
        By lovely devotees,
    So also was the robe that fell
        In folds unto his knees ;
    The graceful apron, too, that hid
        His somewhat sombre frock,
    Was broidered by the fairest kid
        In Bishop Sanzô's flock :
    What wonder that, while such reward
        His pious heart delighted,
    The worthy priest should labour hard
        T' enlighten souls benighted !
Add to this that the Bishop was sturdy and strong,
That his frame was tough, muscular, wiry and long ;
That he stood on his 'pins' just as firm as a rock,
And could stick to a saddle as tight as a 'jock,'
And was always in training, throughout the whole year,
Had the wind of an ostrich, the pace of a deer ;
That he'd tramped it on foot through each neigh-
    bouring clime,

And subsisted on acorns for weeks at a time;
That he shunned beer, tobacco, gin cock-tails, big
    dinners,
Heavy tiffins, and all such delights of weak sinners;
That his features were handsome, his manners were
    mild,
That his voice was as soft as the lisp of a child,
(Here I mean a *good* child, for I hardly need say
When a brat squalls aloud there's the — to pay!)
That his chest it was broad, and his limbs they were
    straight,
That he stood in his sandals just five feet and eight,—
There!—you know Bishop Sanzô, that eminent man,
The most popular preacher in all Hindostan!

 One morn, for reasons good no doubt,
  This jolly priest so sage
 Bestrode his steed, and sallied out
  On pious pilgrimage;
Not the first he had gone, by full many a day,
And this time his steps turned towards the land of
    Cathay.
 Three retainers, bold and true,
  Followed in his rear;
 Quaint they were, and strange to view,
  Yet to him most dear:
 First, a Man of mortal mould,
 Ne'er did puzzled eye behold
  Flunkey half so queer;
 Foremost he of all the band,
 Brandishing with ready hand
  Crescent-headed spear:—

THE BISHOP AND HIS RETAINERS.

Next, there stepped a wondrous shape;
'Twas a most gigantic Ape,
　　Whom the Bishop's fame
Had, from out his forests wild,
Lured, and rendered meek and mild,
　　Tractable and tame!
Last, there followed in the wake,
Shouldering a lengthy rake,
　　Vassal No. Three;
'Twas a Dog of stature great,
Marching, with an air sedate,
On his hind legs, tall and straight
　　E'en as soldier free!
Each in sombre garb was drest,—
Sable jerkin, ditto vest
Edged with gold, black leather belt,
'Butcher boots' of sable felt :—
In the van the master rode,
Close behind the vassals trode,—
Thus their journey they began,
Bishop, Monkey, Dog and Man.

Brightly opes the fair morning, up rises the sun;
See! his rays gild the hills as his race is begun;
Even "Black Cloud" itself, 'neath that glorious light,
Loses half the weird aspect it wore over-night,
　Till, in fact, you're inclined, as the landscape you
　　　view,
Ev'ry ominous tale to regard as untrue.
So, no doubt, thinks our worthy old clerical friend,
As he slowly prepares yonder ridge to descend;

While his steed, and the Monkey, the Dog, and the Man,
With an eye of approval the scenery scan;—
Wait a moment, good sirs,—round the base of that hill,
Straight before you's a sight that's more marvellous still—
Hark! a yelp from the Dog, from the Bishop a cry,
As a Palace superb greets their wondering eye!
    Ne'er did human hands erect
      Palace such as here,—
    Ne'er did mortal architect
      Such a mansion rear!
    Stares the Bishop, struck with dread,—
    Dog and Man would fain have fled,—
    E'en the Monkey shakes his head,
      Thinks it rather queer!
—'Tis a marvellous structure, indeed, to behold;—
Ev'ry timber is fastened with rivets of gold;
From the roof to foundation with jewels 'tis deck'd,
Gleaming bright as the sunbeams whose rays they reflect;
All the tiles are of ivory, polished with care;
All the beams, posts, and rafters of satin-wood rare;
And, in fact, gentle Reader, I'll boldly declare
That, so far as my own slender knowledge goes, ne'er
    Did a scared human eye
    Such a Palace descry
As the Bishop and Co. now before them espy!
—But no noise of a footstep is heard in its halls,
Not a single face looks from its glittering walls,
All is silent and still as the sepulchre, and a
Silken veil quite shuts in e'en the spacious verandah!

THE ENCHANTED PALACE.

  Hark! a weird, a solemn air,
   Notes of music sweet!
  Fairy music, such as ne'er
   Mortal ears did greet!
  Soft, celestial, dulcet strain,
   Fascinating sound!
  Loud it swells, and peals amain,
   Echoes far around!
While the Bishop—good soul! all whose musical skill
Was confined to the banjo or tin-whistle shrill;
Who delighted to list to the wild stirring tones
That a *gamin's* deft hand can evoke from the
  "bones;"
And who loved e'en the tom-tom or Indian drum—
Stands as still as a post, as a statue as dumb!
There he lingers, enraptured and awe-struck and
  dazed:—
Sudden sinks the weird tune,—'fore his vision amazed
Slowly, softly, the long silken curtain is raised!

If the *outside* be gorgeous, what words can avail
To describe the yet further magnificent scale
Of th' apartment *within!*—here I frankly will own
That I *can't* do it justice;—I'll leave it alone,
And beseech you to picture the scene, Reader kind,
For yourself, as may best suit your fanciful mind!
  Yet this much will I tell—
  As the dull oyster-shell
Is outshone by the pearls in its bosom that dwell,—
  As the rich fruity part
  Of a raspberry tart
Is more dear than the crust to a juvenile heart,—

Even so with this Palace—(no metaphor thin)—
By so much is its *outside* surpassed by its *in!*

"Lovely woman," we know, has from earliest times
Ever proved a stock theme for the troubadour's rhymes;
Choose out *any* poems, pick out *any* name,—
Love, Ladies, and Liquor—'tis *always* the same!
  And you'll speedily see
  E'en my Pegasus free
Will ere long take a flight at each one of the three.
—*Place aux dames!*—(for to yield them the *pas* I am
  bound)—
As the Bishop stands staring, and glued to the ground,
Softly rings a sweet voice,—(in a trice he's astir!)—
"You are heartily welcome, right reverend sir!
"Do repose for awhile, in yon arbour pray seat you;
"Both myself and my ladies are happy to meet you!"

  No doubt you've heard the legend told
  How once, in bygone days of old,
   A Saint, by virtue fired,
  Withstood temptation's subtle wile,
  Though shown in most enticing style,
  But scorn'd th' alluring maiden's smile,
   And all unscathed retired:
  Yet had that callous anchorite
  But viewed what greets our Bishop's sight,
   I'll wager even he
  (Unless a very iceberg grown)
  Had somewhat changed his steadfast tone,
  Nor e'er to us the fame been known
   Of "blest St. Anthony!"—

From the Palace emerges a beautiful tribe
Of fair damsels, whose charms I can scarcely describe;
For such figures, such faces, such elegant mien,
I'll confess I have dreamt of, but never have seen!
      Their complexions are fair,
      And their glossy black hair
Is adorned with long tortoise-shell hair pins, so rare
They would cause any jeweller blankly to stare.
Their bewitching, soft eyes are quite coal-black in hue,
(For myself, I must own, I prefer 'em of blue)
And their figures, slight, supple and *not* over big,
Are as lissome and lithe as a willow-tree's twig!
Each is clothed in silk raiment of quality fine,
Where the fanciful hues of the rainbow combine
To produce such a glowing and charming effect
That 'twould seem—but, kind Reader, you scarce can
    expect
That a bachelor bard should be able as yet
To describe as is fitting a lady's toilette!
So I " pass ;"—ev'ry damsel's white finger-tips hold
A long spindle, whose staff is of burnished red gold,
With a top-knot of delicate fine cotton thread
Wound about a light framework that's fixed on the
    head.
—In advance, with a somewhat imperious mien,
Moves a lady whose age might perhaps be eighteen;
By the deference shown her it well may be seen
That the others regard her as being their Queen:
She is ten times as charming, ten times better drest,
And a hundred-fold lovelier, too, than the rest!
She it is whose sweet voice called the travellers nigh,
And she now stands awaiting the Bishop's reply,

While her maidens, with mischievous mirth in each eye,
Murmur softly, "*Yô koso—!—o hairi nasai!*" [1]

In the good Bishop Sanzô's kind heart-strings one spot
For *les dames* had been ever remarkably hot;
He adored lovely eyes, almost worshipped swan-necks—
Was a slave, in a word, to the charms of "the sex!"
    (And, indeed, scandal says
    In the Bishop's young days
He was *rather* addicted to frolicking ways;
And was more than once guilty of conduct quite shady
A propos of some simple, confiding young lady:
—But we'll let the tale rest,—ev'ryone's had his day
In the time of his "hot youth," when Plancus bore sway!)
    So, the spell being broke,
    Th' invitation once spoke,
In a trice he accepts it, turns loose his white 'moke,'
Sits him down on a stool 'neath a sheltering tree,
Nothing loth, so 'twould seem, for a bit of a spree;
Yet, with keen eye to business, his motive so staid is
—"If I could but convert these benighted young ladies!"
Fire away, my good Bishop!—but first let me mention
That they're quite unaware of your pious intention;
And no matter, indeed, though they knew it—I vow
You yourself have more need of conversion just now!

---

[1]. "Welcome! pray enter!"

THE ENCHANTED PALACE.

—Oh! the feast that they tend
To our clerical friend!
There are puddings, cakes, dumplings, and sweets without end!
Then, for fish,—turbots, lobsters, stewed oysters, fried soles!
And delicious raw *daikon*, and delicate rolls!
Incomparable *saké*, Itami's[2] best brew,
(On the barrel the *kembishi*[3] brand you may view!)
But what ails the good Bishop? his manner so quaint is—
I'll be hanged if he tastes even one of the dainties!
As regards liquor also he's just as refraining,
Puts aside proffered drinks with, "No, thanks; *I'm in training!*"
  Has he chanced to espy
  Any circumstance sly
That has warned him against being 'done in the eye!'
Have those words of the Sage sounded fresh in his ear,
Which remark that 'to danger the wise draw not near?'
  I can't guess, I can't say;
  Be that all as it may,
See! he won't 'wet his whistle' nor 'moisten his clay!'
There he sits on his stool, solemn, silent, and glum,
Watchful, wary, alert, keen and cautious, and dumb:
In his hostess's face, too, 'tis plainly expressed
That she can't quite make out this abstemious guest!

---
2 A village in the province of Settsu, Japan, noted for the excellence of its *saké*.
3. *Kembishi*,—"the sword-blade and diamond," a favorite brand of Itami *saké*.

But though *he* may decline any share in their wassails,
It is *tout au contraire* with his jovial vassals;
   ' Nary' one of the three
   Can resist a good spree,
(After living on acorns how thin they must be!)
So with all the rich viands they gladly make free.
How they swallow the sweetmeats—demolish the fish!
With what bumpers of liquor they wash down each dish!
Soon the mirth grows uproarious—loudly they call,
"Choose your partners!—a dance!—now to open the ball!"
First the Dog takes the floor—on his shaky hind-paws
He goes through a *pas seul* that elicits applause;
Next the Man follows suit with a hornpipe or two;
Then the Monkey and he rattle off a *pas deux;*
And then, lastly, the ladies to join them are drawn,
And they all foot it merrily over the lawn!
Oh, what ogling! what squeezing of fingers! what bliss!
What flirtation! and (must I confess?) what a kiss!
Yes, the Dog misbehaves;—quite forgetting his place,
Tries to clasp the fair Queen in his drunken embrace,
And the Queen—knocks him down with a slap on the face!
Just conceive, if you can, the priest's sad consternation
   That his trusty 'bow-wow,'
   So polite until now,
Should on such short acquaintance attempt osculation!
So that kiss is the climax!—he springs to his feet,
Re-arranges his robes, strides away from his seat,

THE MERRYMAKERS.

And without e'en so much as a word of adieu
Turns the corner, and rides away fast out of view,
While his vassals run after him—now only two,
      For the hound
      On the ground
      In a slumber profound
Lies at length, quite unconscious of sight or of sound!
—For veracity's sake (though the word's scarce polite)
I must own that the Dog's unmistakably 'tight'!

      While the Dog is wrapped in sleep,
      See! the ladies forward creep;—
      Slow and stealthy is their pace,
      Stern and cruel ev'ry face!
      Waving high their spindles long
      Towards the sleeper close they throng—
      Waken, Dog! nor tempt thy fate!
      Waken, ere it be too late!
But the Dog doesn't stir,—there he lies on the ground,
And his merciless foes gather silently round!
      See! the Queen here gives a sign!
      Quick their threads they now entwine
      Round their guest, who lies supine!
      Swift they ply their spindles bright,
      Soon they've tied their captive tight;
      Faster still they spin and wind,
      Faster still the victim bind;
      Like a fly he seems, and they
      Spiders gloating o'er their prey!
Yes, the secret is out!—you will scarce feel surprise
At the news that these damsels, so fair to our eyes,
Are *tarantula spiders* in human disguise!

As the somnolent captive's dragged off to their prison,
See! the Man scampers back with lugubrious " phiz "
    on,
    Just to see what's become
    Of his *ci-devant* chum—
At the sight he stands horror-struck, nerveless and
    dumb!
        And alack!
        In a crack
        He sustains the attack
And th' assault of the whole diabolical pack!
How he shrieks! how he struggles with might and
    with main
To escape from the toils!—he may tug, he may strain,
But he can't slip the cords that encompass his
    throttle—
In a moment he's trussed like a second blue-bottle!
    Hark! with harsh, forbidding grate,
        Stubborn locks give way;
    Slowly opes the creaking gate,
        Yawning for its prey!
    In his breast th' unhappy Man
        Feels his heart's blood freeze;
    Fearsome scene his eyes do scan,
        Awful sight he sees!
    Sight that all his senses dulls,
        Wrings his breast with groans—
    Rows on rows of grinning skulls,
        Piles of bleaching bones!
Now, alas! the whole horrible myst'ry's unravelled!—
All those skulls once belonged to ' globe-trotters ' who
    travelled

Over "Black Cloud,"—those bones at some previous
    time, it
May be guessed, were the shins of the folks who *would*
    climb it!
And the Dog and the Man may right well feel
    dejection
At the prospect of adding to such a collection!
What is that?—what the sound that now strikes on
    our ear?
'Tis the tramp of a horse urg'd to headlong career!
Near and nearer it comes!—ere a word can be spoke,
Down the glen gallops wildly the Bishop's white
    'moke.'
How his rider is working, with whip and with rein!
How he 'shoves in the Latchfords' with might and
    with main!
Why, he seems in no whit less determined a state
Than a jock in the ruck turning into the straight!
 Close behind the Monkey springs,
 Bounds as though possessed of wings;
 Wields aloft his iron crook,
 (Something like a fireman's hook),
 Shouts, and howls, and yells amain,
 Strives his master to detain!
 Sanzô little recks or hears,
 Nought regards his vassal's fears,
 Scarcely heeds the frantic cry
 "Bishop! Bishop! *abunai!*"[4]

Darkness closes around! for an instant the hill
Is obscured from our sight—all is silent and still:

---

4. "Beware!"

Then a crash as of thunder resounds through the air,
Bright and vivid there flashes the lightning's weird
    glare!
Peal on peal rolls above us—while loudly around
Mingled shrieks, pray'rs and groans all our senses
    confound,
Savage yells and wild war-whoops incessantly sound!
(It reminds one, in fact, of those dreadful *mêlées*,
—Which delighted us muchly in childhood's sweet
    days—
Such as Fenimore Cooper so aptly describes
As of common occurrence 'mongst Indian tribes!)
   Now each flash of the light-
   ning affords a brief sight
Of the ups and the downs of a desperate fight,
Where the Bishop and Monkey are fiercely beset
By a crew of grim demons, with faces of jet,
Gleaming tusks, and red eye-balls, and long hairy
    paws
That are garnished with bunches of nasty black claws!
   The Bucephalus white,
   Fairly maddened by fright,
Snorts and screams, bucks and plunges and jibs—
    but as tight
As a leech to his back the good clerico sticks,
Holding on by the mane and the pommel "like
    bricks!"
While the Monkey, unscared by the vicious attacks,
Stands his ground, and his master most gallantly
    backs;
   Come one, come all,
   They can't appal!

THE BISHOP IN DANGER.

Quick as thought the smart strokes of his weapon
        now fall!
One he hits on the nose, trips a second one flat,
Punches this in the eye, 'puts a head' upon that,
Whacks a fifth on the ribs, brains a sixth at a
        blow,
'Taps their claret,' and 'rattles their ivories,' so
That they sheer off awhile;—like a shaft from the bow
            The good Bishop 'makes tracks,'
            And his foes being lax,
He has burst through their ranks 'in a couple of
        cracks,'
Spurs his charger, and flies "over bank, bush, and
        scaur,"
In a style unsurpassed e'en by "young Lochinvar!"
(That's a rider who, if the tale's true that we're told,
Was a first-flight performer 'cross country of old,
And who "lifted" his bride like a lamb from the
        fold!)
Sauve qui peut! he scarce thinks, as careering he
        goes,
That he's left the poor Ape in the hands of his foes!

            Light dawns upon the mountain side;—
                No Palace greets our eyes!
            Where once it stood in all its pride,
                Now crags and boulders rise!
            Vanish'd the hall—the ladies fled—
                A dismal pile of rocks
            That rears aloft its rugged head
                Alone our vision mocks!

> Yet o'er that huge dark mass is spread
>   A net, of texture fine,
> E'en as the web the spider's thread
>   So cunningly doth twine.

To be brief, you the sombre exterior view
Of the larder (or gaol) of the devilish crew,
Where our friends lie confined, in as dismal a state
As is fitting in view of their probable fate!

> Hark! from 'neath the granite thick
>   Muffled strokes resound;
> Strokes as of a miner's pick
>   Plying underground!
> Louder yet, and nearer still—
>   Blow succeeding blow—
> Some one's working with a will
>   In the cave below!
> Harder yet we hear him hit;
>   (Practised hand, and deft)
> Crack! the massive rock is split,
>   Right in sunder cleft!

With a whoop of delight, and a wild somersault,
See! the Monkey bounds forth from the grim charnel vault,
Rends the web, and ne'er pausing the fragments to scan,
'Cuts his stick'—he is free! they may catch him who can!

With a leap that would make e'en an acrobat stare,
Up aloft springs the Monkey, and sails through the air!
His gyrations are wonderful—upward he flies,
Soaring high as a lark on its flight to the skies!

(Yet it's not quite a *flight* in the true sense with him,
But a style that's a cross 'twixt a run and a swim,
With a *soupçon*—no more—of the swing that's applied
By an athlete when taking his hurdles ' in stride!')
        As he paddles through the air
        From his chest he plucks the hair,
        Sows it broadcast to the wind,
        Right and left, in front, behind;
And the wondrous results that succeed to this action
Cause us blankly to stare in profound stupefaction:
('Tis the Grand Transformation Scene, here I may
    say,
That is always considered the gem of this play).
        Ev'ry hair that falls to earth
        Gives an infant monkey birth!
        Legions of fantastic shapes,
        Crowds of tiny baby apes,.
        Sudden rise from none knows where,—
        Each the ditto of his *père!*
        Wielding each an iron prong
        On in countless hordes they throng,
        Jumping like so many shrimps—
        Mirth-provoking little imps!
" Children! listen to me!" here the Monkey does say,
" There is *work* to be done—real labor, no play!
" In the dungeon beneath yonder mountain of gran-
" ite there languish two pris'ners, the Dog and the
    Man:
" Set them free! that's the task you are bound to
    fulfil—
" Close your ranks, then! quick march! fall to work
    with a will!"

With a yell of defiance, a howl of delight,
See! the juvenile army swarms on to the fight!
So determined they seem, that we safely may guess
That their efforts ere long must be crown'd with
    success :—
But alas! we're not favored with sight of the fun—
For the curtain here falls—and my fairy tale's done!

I can hardly conceive that my Readers require
Any comments of mine on this tragedy dire.
You may guess for yourselves how the good Bishop
    cried
With delight when his vassals returned to his side—
    How the Dog, from that day,
    Never, even in play,
Tried to steal a sly kiss from a *demoiselle* gay—
    How the Man, after all
    That had chanced to befall,
Never tasted malt liquors, nor went to a ball—
How the Monkey, too, strove his misdeeds to atone,
Grew devout, and went in for tough reading alone—
How they all sailed on smoothly o'er life's troublous
    tide,
And at last in the odour of sanctity died!
For the mem'ry's still cherished, throughout Hindostan,
Of the Bishop, the Monkey, the Dog, and the Man!

THE FENCING MASTER.

*T*HIS tale is NOT *founded on fact, and is, indeed, only remarkable in that it throws some light on the Japanese law of succession. The general rule was, that the son of the true wife should be the heir, even though he might be younger than the offspring of the concubine; but it cannot be supposed that the latter always submitted tamely to such a decision. It is said, and may well be believed, that this rule gave rise to numberless intrigues in noble families, particularly those of the* HATAMOTO, *and in many cases the quarrel was only settled after blood had been shed. We are, however, happy to observe that the difference of opinion was arranged in a more amicable manner in this present instance.*

The Fencing Master;

From the Original Japanese Play of "Nikaigasa" ("A Pair of Hats"), as Performed at the Saruwaka-machi Theatre, Asakusa, Tôkiô, in October, 1878.

MANY long years ago,—
    Some two hundred or so,
The precise date, alas! I don't happen to know,—
Dwelt in Yedo a person whom ev'ry one knew
As the crack Fencing Master—the agèd Yagiu:
    He was heir to a name
    And a family fame
That unsullied through centuries down to him came;
    He was five-eight in height,
    And stood straight and upright,
Though his face was all wrinkled from age, and as white
As a snowflake his hair;—his complexion was light;
He'd a merry dark eye, spite of tell-tale 'crow's feet';
And a smile and a manner remarkably sweet;
And his face was so kindly, you never would dream
His profession was that of a *maître d' escrime!*

Yet could kindle that glance, and could sparkle that eye,

At the 'clackety-clack' of a trusty *shinaye* ;[1]
And, for all his white hairs and his wrinkled old face,
He could deal the 'pear-splitter'[2] with infinite grace,
Wield the sharp *naginata*[3] with exquisite skill,
Fence with one sword, or two, or (more difficult still)
Use the 'sickle and ball,'[4] or the spear, with a will
And in style that his pupils with envy would fill :—
Through the whole of the realm of Japan there were
    few
Who could e'er hope to rival the gallant Yagiu !

Says a proverb that lately I chanced to discover,—" If lucky at cards, you're unlucky in love ;"
—(I remember a friend of my own, who'd a knack
Of acquiring *sans cesse* the best cards in the pack ;
And whene'er I consented to have 'a small game,'
H'd get ' full hands,' ' four aces,' or ' three of the same,'
    Whilst the best fist that e'er
    Fell to *my* humble share
Was no more and no less than a paltry 'two pair'!
Well, *that man's still unmarried*—I'll venture to say
That he's likely a Cælebs for ever to stay !)—
Mars and Venus, again, though they're closely allied,
Do not *always* jog peaceably on side by side ;
And 'twas thus with my hero—though Fate might afford
Him renown *à propos* of his skill with the sword,
Yet *at home* the poor fellow was fearfully bored

---

1. *Shinaye*,—the Japanese fencing stick, formed of slips of bamboo bound together with catgut and leather.
2. *Nashiwari*, or 'pear-splitter,'—a full hit on the crown of the head.
3. *Naginata*,—a long halberd, formed of a broad sword-blade attached to a spear-shaft.
4. *Kusari-gama*,—lit. 'chain-sickle,' formed of an ordinary Japanese sickle (in shape like a miniature scythe) with a heavy ball of metal attached thereto by a slender iron chain ; the chain and ball are whirled round so as to entangle the adversary's weapon, and the sharp-pointed sickle is used at close quarters.

By a question that ever unsolved would remain;—
What the puzzle was here I'll proceed to explain.

        In Japan
        They've this plan
      For a family man,
When his tribe don't increase as it ought, that he can,
If he wish it, bring home a fresh partner for life
As an 'Acting,' 'Assistant,' or 'Number Two' wife!
       Very nice, you'll agree,
       For *Monsieur le mari*,
Thus avoiding the prospect of dying *s. p.*,
(*Sine prole*, that means—genealogists' word)
Though the *honsai*[5] at times doesn't like it, I've heard;
Then what dire complications may happen, you see,
If the *first* and the *second* spouse cannot agree!
(Ah! there's nought like one sole *placens uxor domi!*)
Or, again, there are other small chances in sight
That may spoil one's domestic felicity quite;
Such a one did arrive to our Mister Yagiu
That it put the old chap in a terrible stew.
'Twould appear that our hero, right early in life,
Had been pleased to bring home a most charming
      young wife;
'Twas a love-match,—their tiffs and their quarrels
      were few;
But alas! the weeks, months, and e'en years swiftly
      flew,
And there still were no signs of a little Yagiu!
        Most annoying, 'tis true—
        Nought was left him to do

---

5. *Honsai*,—real wife.

THE FENCING MASTER.

Save to follow the custom I've mentioned above,
And, in short, to seek out and secure a fresh love;
So one day Mrs. Y., to her pain and disgust,
Found herself superseded—aside she was thrust
By a smart little *geisha*,[6] bewitching and flashy,
From a tea-house alongside the Riôgoku-bashi:[7]
Time elapsed, and at length, to the Fencer's great joy,
He became the proud *père* of a fine little boy!
   Whereupon 'Number One,'
   Not to be thus outdone,
Did her best in *her* turn,—ere a twelvemonth had run,
She had *also* presented her lord with a son!
Now of course you'll perceive, from this ample
  digression,
What it was that occasioned the father's depression,
'Twas, in fact, but the thoughts of the law of
  succession;
   For, though equally dear,
   It was none the less clear
That but *one* of the youngsters he'd got on his hands
Could inherit his title and mansion and lands;
And so equal a love did he feel for the pair,
That he *could'nt* select either one as his heir:
Whereupon the mammas for a verdict did press,
Each, of course, with an eye to *her* baby's success,
And so loud waxed the strife that their lord, in a rage,
Vowed at last, with an oath, that he'd make no
  engage-
ment at all in the matter, but quietly wait,
And commit the decision to time and to Fate!

---

6. *Geisha,*—a singing girl.
7. A famous bridge in Tôkiô.

Meanwhile, the sturdy bantlings twain,
    The source of all this ill,
Wax'd fat and big, and throve amain,
    As healthy babies will;
They filled their father's heart with glee
    (He loved domestic joys)—
Upon my word, you'd seldom see
    Such chubby little boys!
(Master Jiubei the elder was named, I should state;
Mataichirô he who'd arrived rather late.)
    And when to childhood's morning-tide
        Did boyhood's noon succeed,
    They ne'er their parentage belied,
        But proved their birth and breed;
    And though, perchance, they often strove,
        And quarrel followed play,
    When all was o'er, fraternal love
        Again resumed her sway!
Then, just fancy their gallant old guv'nor's delight
When they grew up to manhood, so clever and bright,
So accomplished, so handsome, so fair to the sight!
Oh! what pleasure, what pride, and what rapture he felt
When they first swaggered forth with two swords at their belt!
How he taught them to fence! and how apt they became!
How they studied each trick of the dangerous game!
How they toiled ev'ry cut, thrust, and parry to learn,
Every feint, ev'ry guard, ev'ry counter in turn!
Till, at last, as his precepts they'd strictly obey,
Not a man in the realm could fence better than they;

They could 'see' all their chums, 'nary' one was their
    match,
And in each *gekikenkwai*[8] they started at 'scratch'!
Then, of course, these young noblemen, *more suorum*,
Were at times not averse to a breach of decorum;
Each could drink like a fish, when the liquor did flow,
And they never gave in under less than three *shō*[9] —
They could gamble and brawl, and could swagger and
    fret—
And could flirt with each pretty young damsel they met—
And could turn a good verse, and could write it with
    care,
And present it with grace to a singing-girl fair :—
Not a soul with their dash, wit, or learning could vie;
Though you searched Japan over, you never would spy
Such a brace of gay, reprobate young *samurai!*
But, of course, this same gambling and flirting and
    drinking
Made their yearly allowances vanish 'like winking';
So at last they resolved to lead steadier lives,
And, in proof of contrition, took unto them wives;
    This was all very nice,
    'Twas arranged in a trice,
For their sire was quite willing his offspring should
    'splice';
Yet, the nuptials well over, but little space was it
Ere the skeleton once more stepped out of its closet!
    For you'll readily see
    And agree, too, with me,

---

8. *Gekikenkwai,*—a fencing tournament, in which the competitors engage in pairs; the winners are then pitted against each other, until one only remains, who is declared the victor.

9. 1 *shō*—about 3 Imperial pints.

That in view of the probable chances that *three*
Generations might ere long be on the *tapis*,
Worthy Mr. Yagiu ought to set matters square
By selecting, for certain, one son as his heir;
But he *couldn't* yet do it—he shuffled and waited,
Put the evil day off, lingered, procrastinated,
Ever hoping, 'gainst hope, that some providence kind
Would enable him shortly to make up his mind;—
Like Micawber (or me, too, when hunting a rhyme)
He was "waiting for something to turn up" in time!

And it *did*, with a vengeance!—ere married a year
Master Jiubei's behaviour became rather queer;
   Hour on hour would he stare
   With a strange, vacant air,
Quite regardless of aught that was said by his *père*,—
Then he next took to wearing long straws in his hair,—
Rolled his eyes till you'd see nothing else than the white,—
Put his wife, poor O Tei, in the deuce of a fright
By declaring hobgoblins attacked him each night,—
Snatched his dirk from its sheath in a manner unpleasant, [10]
And endangered the lives of the company present,—
Till, to wind up the sum of each wonderful antic,
He one day drove his agèd old father half frantic
By *forgetting his sword* [10] when he passed from the room!
How the Fencer did rave, weep with passion, and fume

---

10. Two of the gravest breaches of etiquette of which a Japanese gentleman under the old *régime*, could possibly be guilty.

JIUBEI'S MADNESS.

At the thought that a son of the house of Yagiu
Such a simply preposterous action should do,
And should sully his name and his lineage high
By a crime so unworthy a true *samurai!*
      Clearly something was wrong—
      He had waited too long
As it was—so he called in the doctor with speed,
And besought his assistance the riddle to read;
But alas! he too soon learned what ailed the poor lad,
The physician confirmed his forebodings so sad—
Master Jiubei, his first-born, was stark staring *mad!*

Fully three years have flown, swift and silent, away,
Yet no change has occurred in the plot of our play!
And the Fencer at noon is reclining at ease,
With his family round him, enjoying the breeze
And the view of his garden's choice flowers and trees,
When a servant flies in, calls his master by name,
And announces an Envoy of rank and of fame
From my lord the Shôgun, with a message of state—
"Show him in!" cries the Fencer—a moment they wait,
    Then the door's opened wide,
    And with solemn slow stride
Now the Envoy stalks in, and sits down at his side:—
" You are welcome, my lord!—I would fain learn from you
" What His Highness may need from the house of Yagiu!"

Right quickly, with a gallant air,
    The Envoy's mission's told;
" His Highness sendeth greeting fair
    " To you, his vassal bold!
" Late yesternight, in Yedo's town
    " Arrived from Kiushiu's strand
" A fencer—one of wide renown
    " Throughout that distant land;
" He bore Us letters from the lord
    " Of Kumamoto's " clan,
" And boasts himself the surest sword
    " E'er known in all Japan;
" If this be so We'd fain decide,
    " And thus We seek to know
" If none be here to tame the pride
    " Of haughty Unshirô;
" And therefore it is Our command
    " And Our decided will
" That bold Yagiu should try his hand
    " With him to test his skill! "

" Ah! my lord," cries the Fencer, in accents of woe,
" Had I but had this chance twenty summers ago
" I'd have seized it with pleasure, and never said 'no'!
" But alas! I'm now agèd—my locks they are white,
" And my legs they are shaky, and dim is my sight;
" I can scarce walk abroad—much less stand up to
    fight!
" I would venture to beg, then, this boon at your
    hands,—
" Let my boy, in my stead, undertake the commands

---

11. Kumamoto, the seat of the Hosokawa family, was the chief castle town of the province of Higo, in the Island of Kiushiu.

"Of His Highness!—he's skilful of fence, is my son,
"And a right pretty blade—"; quoth the Envoy,
              "'Tis done!
"For the youth may well claim to appear thus for
        you,
"In that he also comes of the tribe of Yagiu!"
          Time and place are arranged,
          Bows and smiles interchanged,
And the Envoy takes leave, stalking off as before,
While the household attend him as far as the door,—
All except Master Jiubei, who carelessly sprawls
On the mats, staring up at the flies on the walls!
In this strange occupation he's presently found
When his kinsfolk re-enter and gather around.

"Look at *him!*" groans the Fencer, with sorrowful
        wail;
"Oh! to think that my son his old daddy should fail
"At a time when I most his assistance require!
"Oh! unfortunate youth!—thrice unfortunate sire!"
          Here the wretched old man
          Down his cheeks thin and wan
Pours a deluge of tears—hides his face with his fan—
And (as handkerchiefs then were unknown in Japan)
With his long hanging sleeve dries his eyes and his
        nose;
While the rest, in like fashion, give vent to their woes,
          And so weep, wail, and shout,
          Sob, and tumble about
In their grief, that they kick up the deuce of a rout!—
"Mataichirô!" here says the Fencer,—"my lad,
"You're promoted to act *vice* Jiubei the mad;

"If my first-born, alas! cannot come to the front,
"You, I know, of this combat can well bear the brunt,
"How d'ye feel?"—"Well, I think I'm a match for
    most men,
"And I'll bet I make fully nine hits out of ten!"—
        "Good!" his father replies;
        "Guard against all surprise,
"Keep your sword-point well up in a line with your
    eyes,
"Don't be rash, watch each trick Mister Unshirô tries,
"Just remember my precepts, hit hard, and wire in,
"And I'll lay fifty *yen* [12] to a *tempo* [13] you win!"—
Mataichirô bows at his old father's side,—
Says adieu to O Misa (his lovely young bride),—
Turns to Jiubei, and begs that he'll kindly excuse
Him for having thus coolly stepped into his shoes,—
Takes his leave of the rest,—and then, turning his
    back,
Picks the *shortest* [14] of fencing-sticks out of the rack,
(That's the sign of true swordsmanship, ev'ry one
    knows)
Calls his servant, and forth to the tournament goes.

'Tis a glorious sight, on the morrow's bright morn,
To behold the gay crowd on the Castle's wide lawn;
There the lists they are pitched, and pavilions are
    spread,
And the sawdust is strewn for the fencers to tread,

---

12. 1 yen = rather less than a Mexican dollar.
13. Nearly equal to 1 cent.
14. Alluding to the Japanese fencing proverb, "A quick return is better than a long parry."

And my lord the Shôgun in his dignity sits,
While the gentlemen, soldiers and poets and wits
Of his court throng about him in holiday clothes,
And the gay *hatamoto* are squatting in rows
Betting freely, and wagering jewels and gold
On the relative skill of the combatants bold;
All restraint is abandoned—they're out on the spree,
And appear just as jolly as jolly can be!
    Beneath, apart from all the rest,
        The gaze of each beholder,
    Stands forth a man, in silken vest
        Looped up behind each shoulder,
    And trousers hitched above the knee
        As fencers' statutes show,—
    By mien and dress we well may see
    'Tis Higo's noted swordsman, he,
        The haughty Unshirô!
    His massive biceps is displayed,
        And bared each brawny limb;
    He needs must be a skilful blade
        Who dares encounter *him!*
    Nor waits he long—his sturdy foe
        Now marches into view;
    The heralds loud their conches blow,
    Announcing—" Mataichirô,"
        " The son of old Yagiu!"

Bowing low 'fore the throne, in an accent that's meek
Mataichirô here craves permission to speak:—
" Be it known to your Highness, my father so dear
" By his age and infirmity cannot appear;
" And although my big brother should come in his stead,

"*He*, alas! is prevented—(he's wrong in the head)—
"Thus on *me* it devolves, as the last of the name,
"To uphold your renown and our family fame:
"But alas! I'm incompetent quite for the task—
"Let our friend here 'walk over'—that's all that I ask,
"For I'm simply convinced I could make no pretence
"Of a match 'gainst a foe with his cunning of fence!"
(Here a panic takes place 'midst the gay betting-men,
And our hero goes backward to fifty to ten!)
"Not at all!" roars his rival, with gross disrespect;
"You'd defraud me of victory?—little I reck'd
"That amongst all the swordsmen throughout Yedo town
"There should only be cravens!"—"Shut up, and sit down!"
   Cries the herald;—"Yagiu,
   "Such a course will not do,
"And His Highness commands you at once to set to!"
Mataichirô blushes with joy at this pledge
Of regard,—and the 'bookmakers' hasten to 'hedge'!

  Foot to foot and hand to hand,
  Now the practised swordsmen stand;
  Cautious foes, with courage leal,
  Eyes of fire, and wrists of steel!
  Soon in quick succession fly
  Blow, and thrust, and feint so sly,
  Parry, counter,—now they close,
  Part again, and backward goes
  Either champion full a yard,
  Standing warily on guard,—

THE FENCING BOUT.

Turn, and at it once again,
Ply their single-sticks amain,
Put forth all their skill—in vain!
Nought avails it, not a whit—
Neither one can make a hit!

Round the second!—as before,
Long they strive, though wearied sore;
Then—though fickle, sometimes true—
Fortune seems to aid Yagiu;
Fall his blows like wint'ry rain,
Backward now, and yet again,
He his foeman, pace by pace,
Drives across the listed space
'Gainst the palings 'neath the throne—
Now, proud boaster! hold thine own!
Strive as best thou may'st!—but no,
Nought can check the final blow!
Ha! what's that?—th' uplifted brand
Flies from out the victor's hand—
Falls before him on the sand!
" Disarmed! disarmed!"—the combat's done,
The winner's lost—the loser's won!

Mataichirô bows, and retires from the ground;
Mr. Unshirô stares with surprise all around,
  For he cannot make out
  How a foeman so stout
Should have chucked up his chances of winning the
  bout;
And my lord the Shôgun, too, seems mightily vexed
At the issue, and looks not a little perplexed—

"Ha! I've got it!" at length he cries:—what is't he's got?
—Your indulgence, kind reader! this scene 'sayeth not'!

On the spacious verandah, in view of his gate,
Sits the Fencer, whose mind's in a sad troubled state,
  As he waits the return
  Of his son, ere he learn
All the ups and the downs of the combat so stern.
There he comes!—"Mataichirô! how went the fight?"
Not a word in response—in a terrible fright
(Though he tries to conceal it) he cries, "Oh, my son!
"I'm on tenter-hooks, waiting the news that you've won—
"For you *have* won, I bet—*you* would never be tricked!
"Answer!"—"Well, if I must, I'm—disgracefully licked!"
  With a stupified air
  And incredulous stare,
Here the Fencer sinks down on the matting—and there
He reclines, looking truly more dead than alive,
And as white as I'm painfully conscious that *I*'ve
Look'd, whene'er I 'fell flat' while attempting a dive!
 "*Now*, father dear," the youth does cry,
  "From this you well may see
  "How all incompetent am I
   "Your heir-at-law to be!

"In Jiubei's name your will must run,
   "I'll yield to him with joy;
"Though I'm the son of 'Number One,'
   "He's still your elder boy!
"As for *me*—thus disgraced, I'm unworthy to bear
"E'en the name that belongs to my brother and *père*;
"So I'll change it—turn *chônin* [15]—and get me to work
"At the *soroban*, [16] 'stead of the sword and the dirk!"
—Up he springs, with an air of decision and gloom,
And, as stiff as a drill-sergeant, stalks from the room.

Once again the door opens, and Mister Yagiu
Sees the face of his first-born appear to his view:
Master Jiubei bears in two enormous round hats
Such as farmers wear—these he lays down on the
     mats
Just in such a position as plainly to show
That he's marked on this '*Chiu*,' and on t'other one
     '*Kô;*'
(That is, 'Loyalty,' 'Filial Piety'—these
Are a precept familiar to all Japanese.)
   "Oh, father dear," he murmurs, while
      The Fencer starts in dread,
   "You know how loose is ev'ry tile
      "Upon my hare-brained head!
   "No swordsman I—I scarce can be
      "Your apt successor—so
   "Pray leave th' inheritance from me
      "To Mataichirô!

---

15. Chônin.—lit. 'wardsman'; one of the ordinary townspeople, as opposed to the military class or gentry.

16. Soroban.—the abacus, or counting board used by Japanese merchants in making arithmetical calculations.

"''Tis but his right—you can't but please
    "That justice should be done—
    "Though I'm your elder boy, yet he's
    "The child of 'Number One!'"
"As for *me*—I've resolved to turn farmer, my sire,
"And to toil all day long in the paddy-field mire,
"Rise at dawn, go to bed when the stars twinkle free;
"And if e'er I'm inclined discontented to be,
"Just a glance at these hats, with their mottos so true,
"Will recall what I owe to my brother and you!"

"Oh, you reprobate!" roars his old father, in ire;
"Turn a coolie! dig *daikon!* till 'paddy-field mire!'
"What the deuce do you mean?—do you fancy that *I*
"Could permit for a moment that e'er you should try
"To degrade thus the rank of the true *samurai?*
"Turn a sword into ploughshare!—Turn farmer!—
            But stay,
"You shall use that same sword in a different way;
        "So, my springal so gay,
        "You will please to obey,
"And commit *hara-kiri sans* any delay!
"What! you won't? then I'll pretty soon make
        you!"—and here,
With a snatch he takes down from the wall a long
        spear,
Makes a couple of passes (just testing its weight),
Fiercely glares at his son, and then 'goes for him
        straight!'
            But although he may boast
            That he's still match for most
Men, he finds that he's here reckoned *minus* his host;

THE RIDDLE SOLVED.

Master Jiubei has caught up the hats in a crack,
Whirls them round as a shield 'gainst the Fencer's
    attack,
Makes a dive at the spear-head, and then in a trice
Holds it tightly between them as though in a vice!
How the father does stare, at this marvellous *ruse*
Of his lunatic son!—he consents to a truce—
And in wonder ejaculates—" *Do-o-o-mo !*"—(that's
    ' Zooks !')
" Why, I'm blessed if the fellow's so daft as he looks !"

" Daft ! I never *was* daft !" Jiubei says with a sob ;
" All my lunacy's nought but a long set-up job,
" In the hope that my father, reduced to despair
" By my illness, would choose for successor my *frère* ;
" I'm the elder—but who was my mother ?—I swear
" That no son of a *gonsai* [17] should oust the true heir !"
    E'er this speech is well o'er
    Comes a knock at the door—
Mataichirô enters, and bows to the floor :
    " Dearest *pater !*" cries he,
    " Don't be angry with me
" If I frankly confess what you've failed yet to see—
" I will make a clean breast, and will candidly tell
" That my fencing this morning was nought but a 'sell '—
" Done on purpose—in order that Jiubei might win
" The inheritance, mansion, and title, and ' tin ' !
" I'm the child of your first wife—but still I would
    scorn,
" E'en in view of that fact, e'er to oust your first-born !"

---

17. *Gonsai*,—concubine, as opposed to the *Honsai*, or true wife. Rather a slang term.

Here's a kettle of fish!
Though the Fencer may wish
It, he cannot quite swallow this wonderful dish!
But who comes?—that's a face we recall to our mind—
'Tis the Envoy!—he enters—and slowly behind
Files a train of attendants who solemnly bear
Sundry packages, tied up and labelled with care:
"These are cumshaws," says he, "to the son of Yagiu
"From His Highness, who's pleased to approve of the true
"Skill and free style of hitting you lately displayed—"
"But I lost! I was beaten!"—"Not much, my young blade;
"You were winning right easily when you elected
"To abandon the game—why, your *ruse* was detected
"On the spot, though you strove your intentions to smother—
"All the town knows what's up betwixt you and your brother!
"And His Highness thus graciously marks his esteem,
"For he's not quite so verdant as p'raps you may deem!"—
 "Thanks, noble sir!" in grateful strain
  Exclaims the old Yagiu;
 "Perhaps you'll also kindly deign
  "To say what I should do,—
 "How I should solve this riddle 'mixed,'
  And end this question vext—
 "I'm in a sad quandary fixed,
  "And grievously perplexed!"—
"There's but *one* way," the Envoy replies, "to get out
"Of the matter;—they're equally skilful, no doubt,

THE FENCING MASTER.   135

"With the sword—let them *fence* for the title, and he
"Who the victor may prove your successor shall be!"
"Done!" and "Done!" cry the others; both young-
    sters with zest
Grab their single-sticks, quickly doff mantle and vest,
And, as neither his toilette unduly prolongs,
In a moment they're at it—aye, 'hammer and tongs'!

Now I would that the Muse would inspire me aright
To describe in fit terms this most desperate fight,
    That I truly might tell
    Each event that befel,
The attacks, and the guards, and the counters as well,
As, in fine mimic warfare, each loving young brother
Most fraternally whacked and belaboured the other!
But alas! the fair lady, though willing to tell a
Peaceful story, don't love *bella, horrida bella!*
So I'll cut matters short (as my paper's nigh done)
By announcing that *neither* the victory won—
Not a hit was obtained—and each gallant young man
Merely finished precisely as first he began!—
Here the Envoy speaks forth;—"This tough point,
    I opine,
"Had as well be now settled by judgment of mine:
"I decide, then, for Jiubei—indeed, to my sight,
"The succession is his (as the elder) of right;
"So let *him* be the heir—Mataichirô here
"Is a swordsman unequalled, with never a peer;
"Let him start, like his dad, as a Master of Fence,
"Let him travel through ev'ry wide province, and thence
"Let the fame of his feats reach his own native town,
"Let him win for himself titles, honor, renown,

" Let him prove himself skilful, and gallant, and true,
" And exalt to the heavens the name of Yagiu!"

Curtain falls!—I trust, friends, that this may not be quite
Such a tough job to *read* as I've found it to *write*!

MORAL.

I.

I would warn ev'ry son who may feel the desire
Just to simulate madness to worry his sire,
      To keep open his eyes
      And beware how he tries
To display too much int'rest in bluebottle flies;
For in such case, no matter how sober he be,
All his neighbours will swear that he's in for D. T.!

II.

Worthy 'bruisers'!—to you I'd commend moderation;
Pray do not use your 'mawleys' on slight provocation!
      If a fool should deride
      'Slang' him back on *your* side—
For the tongue's a good weapon when properly plied!
But if e'er you should find that mere words don't retard,
And you *must* hit the fellow—*then*, mind, *hit him hard!*

www.ingramcontent.com/pod-product-compliance
Lightning Source LLC
Chambersburg PA
CBHW020257170426
43202CB00008B/406